D1265714

To those with whom I share my love and who share their love with me, accepting each other for what we are and delighting in each other's interests. To my parents, Nora and Peter; my husband, Bob; and my children, Robert and Anna Mae.

ANNA MAE WALSH BURKE, Ph.D., is also the author of
Are You Ready?: A Survival Manual for Women Returning to School,
and *Computers Can Be Kidstuff*. She has published more than
forty technical articles in professional journals. Dr. Burke has
been a university administrator for several years, and is
currently the director of the Center for Science and
Engineering at Nova University, Fort Lauderdale, Florida. She
has spent considerable time counseling students, both young
and adult, about making transitions in their lives.

ANNA MAE WALSH BURKE

What do you want to be now that you're all grown up?

A SPECTRUM BOOK

Prentice-Hall, Inc., Englewood Cliffs, New Jersey 07632

Library of Congress Cataloging in Publication Data

Burke, Anna Mae Walsh.
What do you want to be now that you're all
grown up?

A Spectrum Book
Includes index.
1. Career changes.   2. Vocational guidance.
I. Title.
HF5384.B87   650.1′4′0240564   81-17938
                                  AACR2

ISBN 0-13-952044-9

ISBN 0-13-952036-8 {PBK.}

This Spectrum Book is available to businesses and organizations at a special
discount when ordered in large quantities. For more information, contact:
Prentice-Hall, Inc., General Publishing Division, Special Sales,
Englewood Cliffs, N.J. 07632

1 2 3 4 5 6 7 8 9 10

Editorial/production
supervision by Alberta Boddy
Cover design by April Stewart
Manufacturing buyer: Cathie Lenard

Prentice-Hall International, Inc., *London*
Prentice-Hall of Australia Pty. Limited, *Sydney*
Prentice-Hall of Canada, Ltd., *Toronto*
Prentice-Hall of India Private Limited, *New Delhi*
Prentice-Hall of Japan, Inc., *Tokyo*
Prentice-Hall of Southeast Asia Pte. Ltd., *Singapore*
Whitehall Books Limited, *Wellington, New Zealand*

Contents

1

Ready for change

CHANGE Have you ever thought of the sound of the word? For me it has a brittle sound. The sound of a battle axe hitting a piece of armor. The sound of a bell breaking the stillness of the night. The sound of a wire snapping, a glass breaking, a brittle sound, the sound of change washes across our lives bringing joy and sadness. Sometimes we choose the change. Sometimes it is the result of other forces.

The rate of change has increased dramatically in our own lifetime. There are individuals who watched men land on the moon in July of 1969 who were alive when Orville and Wilbur Wright made the first flight. The typewriter, a self-contained mechanical device, is a recent invention in the history of mankind. As long as it was in coming, however, the simple manual typewriter has been quickly replaced by the electric machine. Today I am writing this book sitting at my own computer in my own family room. I am using a word processing program so that I can change my words until I am satisfied, and print as many versions of my text as I wish. This is a dramatic change in a short span of years.

Again the word *change*. What place does this word have in your life? There is no doubt that you are going to be affected by change, but there are some things you can do to prepare for it.

When my book *Are You Ready? A Survival Manual for Women Returning to School* was published, a number of men who themselves had returned to prepare for a new career in a college program I had designed asked me to write a book for them too.

"You can secretly read *Are You Ready?*" I would reply with a smile. "I'll put it in a plain brown wrapper so no one will know that you are reading a book I wrote for women." "You can't be chauvinistic," they said. "Remember ERA. We need help too."

Along with the humor came the realization that there was a need to answer some broader questions, and that many of these answers were indeed "non-sexist." For many people, going back to school was a large part of the answer, but indeed it was only part.

Some attention is just beginning to be paid to changing roles for women, but the question of change is an important one for both men and women, today. The times are changing, and they are changing for all.

Whatever your feelings about the women's movement may be, its effect cannot be ignored. It has caused people to focus on various aspects of their lives and relationships. Many men as well as women are beginning to take a serious second look at their lives and lifestyles.

The question that many men and women have to answer is one of a career change. For some, this career change results in a dramatic lifestyle change. For others the change is not so traumatic.

The purpose of this book is to help you explore your life and your interests, identify new careers and goals, and plan for a positive change in your life.

You may have been seriously considering a change in your life. It may only be a nagging restlessness, a secret wish, or it may have taken a stronger form. You may already know what you would like to change.

One of the major changes you may be considering is a change in career. This kind of change has a tremendous impact on your total life. It may affect family relationships or it may change your lifestyle or your finances. It may cause you to move or to go back to school. It may, and probably will, cause changes in every facet of your life. If you are considering a new career, it is important that you plan very carefully. This book has been written to help you make this change a positive experience.

Do not feel that you are alone in thinking about making such a change. Such desires are not new, but it is only under special circumstances that men were able to change careers in days gone by. A serf who was tired of tilling the soil of England and wanted a more adventurous career might have found himself being shipped off to a Crusade. Whether he stayed on the farm or went off to war, the choice was really out of his hands. The lord of his manor made the choice for him. People could not easily rise "above their station."

For you those words are meaningless. In reality a person is limited only by his or her talents and imagination and drive. You may say that this is not so, but you know that it is true. People do get out of the ghetto, poor boys do get to be millionaires, women do get to be doctors and judges as well as movie stars. Not everyone does, but some do succeed.

The person who is making a career change cannot afford to make mistakes. The young person just starting out has, in some respects, nothing to lose. The adult already has a life and a lifestyle. There is always the fearful shadow that the new career, the new life, may not be as good as the old one.

Do you remember the two figures in the painting *American Gothic*? A man and a woman, images of each other, standing side-by-side, a pitch fork held staunchly in front of them, a farm scene behind them. They seem to be the personification of a steady, unchanging life, yet they existed at a time when there was considerable change on the American frontier. People moved from cities and towns in the East to gain a chance in the West. The pioneers were by no means all young. Many were heads of families. For some the journey was a success, for others a failure.

You have the freedom to choose. You may be the solid figure in *American Gothic*, content, unchanging, or you may change and either succeed or fail. Fate cannot take all the credit for your failures. You can tip the odds in your favor by careful choices and careful planning.

Mid-life career change is not a new phenomenon. It is an age-old problem. A few people associate this experience with such intense degrees of fear, regret, depression, and/or anxiety that mental illness has been the result. Psychologists have long used "mid-life crisis" as a descriptive term for this phenomenon. In our world of "pop" psychology, this term has been applied to any one who is considering a change in career, lifestyle, etc. People even apply it to themselves. An apparently well-balanced gentleman with whom I had lunch recently, used the term to fill me in on what he had been doing during the past two years. "I've been having my mid-life crisis," he said. "I changed my wife and my job and went back to school." That isn't a misprint, he really did say wife, not life. I have no way of knowing the degree of trauma he really suffered, but I still have a feeling he meant "change" rather than "crisis."

Change can be good or change can be bad. Mid-life change is no different. Indeed, it may be a mixture of both—a bittersweet process.

Everyone wants to believe that his or her problem is unique. Most people don't want to consider certain aspects of their lives a problem. They do not understand that many suffer the same thoughts they do. They do not understand the process of making a transition. The secret of a successful change lies in the way in which the transition is made.

Many are insecure about the process for making a change. They believe they are alone. They do not understand that many others have gone through the same thing and they do not understand that it can be a good thing. They unconsciously cry out, "don't give me a label or a lecture. Teach me a way to find my own solution." This book is intended to do that.

Stress seems to be a dominant component of American life. To some degree it is a valuable component. There are those who believe that a certain amount of stress is a necessary and valuable part of the successful life. It is important that you learn to control stress. An important aspect of this is minimizing unnecessary tension in your life.

In a classic study done some years ago, psychologists attempted to develop a scale to evaluate stress according to a point system. Too many points indicated that the subject could be in trouble. An important thing to remember is that good and happy things cause stress as well as unhappy things. If we take a look at some of the point ratings on the Holmes-Rahe Scale we will understand better how a career change will dramatically add up the points so that your life may reach a crisis stage.

The most traumatic experience identified by the study, the death of a spouse, is rated at 100 points. (see Table 1). Divorce was close behind. A major change in arguments with spouse is a 35. Financial changes are also high. A wife starting or ending work is a 26, major changes in family get-togethers is a 15, failure is a 43, outstanding personal achievement is a 36, beginning or end of formal schooling is a 27, illness is a 44. A number of the scores were work related. Being fired is a 47, retirement a 45, business adjustment a 39, change to a different line of work a 36, major change in work responsibilities a 29, trouble with the boss a 23, major change in working conditions a 20.

Table 1 Social Readjustment Rating Scale

Rank	Life Event	Mean Value
1	Death of a Spouse	100
2	Divorce	73
3	Marital separation	65
4	Jail term	63
5	Death of a close family member	63
6	Personal injury or illness	53
7	Marriage	50
8	Fired at work	47
9	Maritial reconciliation	45
10	Retirement	45
11	Change in health of family member	44
12	Pregnancy	40
13	Sex difficulties	39
14	Gain of new family member	39
15	Business readjustment	39
16	Change in financial state	38
17	Death of a close friend	37
18	Change to different line of work	36
19	Change in number of arguments with spouse	35
20	Mortgage over $10,000	31
21	Foreclosure of mortgage or load	30
22	Change in responsibilities at work	29
23	Son or daughter leaving home	29
24	Trouble with in-laws	29
25	Outstanding personal achievement	28
26	Wife begins or stops work	26
27	Begin or end school	25
28	Change in living conditions	20
29	Revision of personal habits	24
30	Trouble with boss	23
31	Change in work hours or conditions	20
32	Change in residence	20

Table 1 Social Readjustment Rating Scale (continued)

Rank	Life Event	Mean Value
33	Change in schools	20
34	Change in recreation	19
35	Change in church activities	19
36	Change in social activities	18
37	Mortgage or loan less than $10,000	17
38	Change in sleeping habits	16
39	Change in number of family get-togethers	15
40	Change in eating habits	15
41	Vacation	13
42	Christmas	12
43	Minor violations of the law	11

Source: Holmes, T.H.,and Rahe, R.H. The Social readjustment rating scale. Journal of Psychosomatic Research,1967,11, 213-218.

I have selected only some of the stress-triggering situations that may develop as a result of a career change. You can even collect a number of points by only "thinking " about changing careers. Holmes-Rahe used 300 points collected over a period of a couple of years as a critical number. Think of all the points you could be adding up. There may be family difficulties, you may have financial changes, you may both begin and end school, you may have difficulties with wife, in-laws, parents, children or friends. You may get all the work-related points. You may get points for both failure and success. I think you must have the idea by now. Changing careers is a very stressful activity. You must minimize your stress components if you are to maximize your chance for success.

Change is a process of gain and loss. Part of the process of selecting a new career is a thorough estimate of what you will gain and what you will lose. Do the gains outweigh the losses, not just in number but also in quality? Can you live without the things you will be surrendering?

Change implies transition. You do not wake up one morning with everything instantly changed. Pieces of your life will change at different rates. Something old, something new, something borrowed, something blue. Some people cannot face the transitions. Some people cannot survive them. Planning the change means planning transition.

How do you know if you are ready? If you are to be ready for change you must understand many things about yourself, your present life, and your relationships. Perhaps most importantly, you will have to make a very careful choice of a new career.

2

Now that you're all grown up

How many times when you were a child, were you asked, "What are you going to be when you grow up?" Someone may have pinched your cheek while posing the question and your answer may have been mixed with wishing you were somewhere else.

Can you remember your answer? Did it come true? Did you really think about it? Did you ever really think about it—or did you just grow up and get a job? Did you plan your life or did it just sort of happen?

Remember the childhood games—"rich man, poor man, beggar-man, thief, doctor, lawyer, Indian chief." Looking back, the words now sound more like the characters in a pop-rock group. The choices of careers for men as well as women were often as limited as the words in that game.

Many of the choices were jobs, not careers. They were for the most part the same categories of jobs that the people around you were engaged in. It was not necessarily a matter of following in your father's (or mother's) footsteps. It was a matter of knowing and of having opportunities. Was there even a way for you to find out about the different kinds of careers that were available?

Words are interesting, powerful tools for understanding more about ourselves. The difference between the word *job* and the word *career* is an ocean of pride, income, and sometimes independence. Let us explore Webster's Intermediate Dictionary (1977 edition) for the meanings of the word *job* and the word *career*.

A job is defined as a duty or a task, or a position at which one regularly works for pay. A career is a profession pursued as a permanent calling. A career is alternately defined as a course of continued progress or activity. The first two definitions are what you might expect. It is the third one that is really important to us.

When I use the word *career* I mean it in a much broader sense than just the destination of a few professions such as law, teaching, nursing, and medicine. On a day-to-day basis a career is a job, but continued movement and development is inherent in it. A career generally has many stages which may differ in degree of responsibility, creativity, complexity, financial reward, or some characteristic intrinsic to the position. When I use the word *career* in the remainder of the book, I mean it in this broader sense. When you select a new career, think of all the stages. Look at them at perhaps five-year intervals. What will you be doing five, ten and twenty years from now, if you choose a particular career. Does that career have a single track or are there many places in which the career can branch? What kinds of decisions must be made at the branch points? Do all of them lead to things which you like to do? Because we cannot accurately predict the future, this may seem to be a futile task but some effort must be made to project the future stages of the career you select. How stable are those career areas in the technologically volatile world in which we live?

Some individuals who are reading this book have been forced to change careers because the jobs they currently hold are being phased out. If that job was a link in a career chain the career itself may have taken a completely different turn or have been terminated. The most recent material which I have read indicates that college graduates may expect to have two or three different careers in a lifetime. Some people do not think of themselves in terms of a career, but it is important that they begin to do so. Just "holding a job" becomes increasingly difficult in today's world. Inflation is rarely met by cost of living raises and merit raises are almost non-existent. The principal process for financial movement seems to be movement on the career ladder.

The questions about financial improvement bring up new areas for questions and a new term. What are your professional goals? Your goals are your objectives, the things which you would like to achieve. A good salary, having a number of people report to you, freedom to design your own projects, and an ability to work independently are all examples of professional goals. These goals may be translated into specific positions on the career ladder you have choosen. You may want to be a vice-president or a head designer or a lawyer with a private practice. You will have to establish some professional goals as well as select a specific career.

Men are often asked, "What do you do for a living?" Women are still more likely to be asked if they are married, if they have children, or possibly, where they work. The association of the word *career* with the word *woman* is not readily made by either men or women. Whether you are a man or a woman, you must associate the word *career* with yourself rather than just having a job. Don't ever think it is too late!

What did we know, you and I, about choosing a career when we were growing up? Nobody even called it a *career* when I was growing up. It was, "what would I" be?

But in the end *being* is a much larger question than we shall try to answer here. The selection of a new career may indeed be part of the creation of a new self and a new self-image.

In some respects self and self-image cannot be separated as demonstrated by the rather broad range of questions asked below. The use of the answers however will be limited to the selection of a new career. Although you may have many ideas occur as a result of the questions presented later in this chapter, the essential question that we will focus on and which you must answer for yourself is "Now that I am all grown up, what do I want to be?"

Where do you start thinking about this? Are you satisfied with your current job ? Is it just a job or does it have some elements of a *career* as defined above? Do you believe that what you do every day is what you really want to do? If someone asks you what you do, how do you feel when you answer?

Try this test question. If you were a guest on a television program and had to tell the whole country what you do for a living, how would you feel? How would you describe your job? What would you call it? Would you be proud, ashamed, embarrassed or just neutral? Are you able to describe your job to other people? What words do you use to tell others what you do? Are there some parts of your job that you like? Are there some parts that are exciting to you?

Let us move to a key question:

What Do You Really Want to Be Now That You're All Grown Up?—Take a look at all those words.

WHAT

Do you really know—are there dreams to be reckoned with—?
How do you know which career is the right one for you?
How can we find out?
Are there things you never thought of?
Did the right career for you even exist when you were starting out?
In the case of many, especially women, are you only really starting out now?
Have you been holding jobs and now want to move to the broader concept of a career?

DO (is an action word)

What are you able to do?
What are your abilities?
What kind of change can you carry out?
What kind of changes are you really willing to carry out?

YOU

Who are you?
Have you ever really thought about yourself?
How do you describe yourself?
How do others describe you, your family and your friends.
Are there things that you would like to change about yourself?
Are these things external changes or internal changes?
How do you go about changing yourself?

REALLY WANT TO BE

What kind of things do you like to do?
What kind of new careers would you like to explore?
How do you find out about new kinds of work?
How do you prepare for them?
Would you really like them?
What kind of a change would they make in your life?
Would you like that change?

NOW THAT YOU'RE ALL GROWN UP

What does it mean to be an adult?

Are there certain things that are different because you are an adult?

What kinds of responsibilities cannot be changed in your life?

What would a career change mean in your life?

For many, Paul Gauguin represents the mid-life change. He went from being an ordinary man with a wife and child and a job in an office to being an artist on the island of Tahiti, a life free and unbounded. For some people, this would seem to be the ideal life. They do not necessarily want to paint under the breadfruit trees, but may be seeking to escape responsibility and lives that have become very mundane. Others may be afraid to even consider a change because they feel it implies a desire to run away. These people are not seeking to avoid responsibility but secretly want to find a career, and ultimately a life, that is more satisfying. They may be afraid family or friends will think they are trying to escape responsibility. They may even be secretly afraid that they *are* trying to escape responsibility, themselves.

People who dream of Tahiti may need a certain amount of courage, but they do not need to make the kind of plans we will be discussing. Those who are concerned about finding balance in their lives will find that they need to plan any change very carefully.

The question of being *grown up* is one that deserves some exploration. What does it mean to be an adult? What is the first thing that pops into your mind? If you ask a teenager, you might get an answer that focused on driving a car. If you asked a person burdened by responsibilities, the answer might focus on that aspect.

In fact, adulthood has four aspects, and they certainly don't happen to us simultaneously. The first is the biological definition of adulthood—the time when you have the ability to reproduce. This definition comes into effect years earlier than any of the other definitions.

The second is a legal definition. The laws for marriage, the draft, driving, drinking, voting, making contracts, etc. designate various ages for the legal definition of adulthood and may vary from state to state and from country to country, yet all take the position of relating legal adulthood to a specfic age.

The third definition links adulthood to the sociological aspects of man. When do you start performing adult roles, such as worker, citizen, family head, father, mother? This definition is extremely important in a career change. The process of change may result in your moving to what might be considered a "non-adult" role for a period of time, for example, that of student or apprentice. You have a certain sociological aspect to your life. You may be a respected member of your community because of what you do. Will this be maintained in the career change? Will your sociological aspect be enhanced? Initially? Ultimately?

The fourth definition of adulthood is a psychological one. Do you think of yourself as an adult? This question may be especially important for women who entered a home role at an early age and have not functioned as an adult in certain psychological or sociological ways.

Whether you are conscious of it or not, as an adult you have established a set of values for yourself and your life. These values may have a moral component or they may be related to religious feelings and feelings concerning morality. They may have an economic component, relating to money and the things money can buy. They may have a personal component which is related to the manner in which you interact with people and even the fact that some people are important to you. What is important to you? Who is important to you? What is most important? Yourself, other people, things you create, money, power, God. Everyone has a list and the list changes according to the circumstances. What would you do to get what? This is where your personal set of values comes into place. You will have to think about your set of values. They will be important when setting your professional goals. How will you decide what will be important in the selection of a new career?

What is your perception of yourself? Are you happy with yourself as an adult? Self-analysis is very difficult, even when it is limited to the question of career choice. How do you look when you stand back and hold yourself out at arms length? Will you avoid some answers to certain questions because you are afraid of them? Have you been avoiding certain topics with regard to yourself for years? Have you created some buffers so that you do not have to admit certain things to even yourself? It will be important to try, to begin with yourself. If this does not seem to be working, you may have to turn to professional help. For some individuals, a career change is a way of changing their total life, of growing up again. The *why* you want a new career is something you will discover for yourself as we move through the process of identifying a new career and the way to achieve it.

If you have a habit, as I do, of checking magazine counters to see what is being published you may find articles with checklists and little self-surveys that will tell you what is wrong with your life, or what is right with your life, or what color you should dye your hair, etc. Some of these articles and questionaires are quite useful, not only because of the information contained there, but also because they make you consider certain questions in relation to your own life.

I don't believe in giving point values to things and adding up your life like a bingo game, but I do believe it is possible to draw out some things you may have even been unaware of through the use of lists. The creation of different lists will be an important part of the process of identifying a new career and taking the necessary steps to achieve your goals.

Take yourself, a pad of paper and a pencil to a quiet, comfortable place where you will not be interrupted or under any constraints of time. You may not be able to finish this exercise in one sitting. It is probably better if you come back to it several times and refine your lists over and over. Remember that you are planning your future, and possibly that of your family. Do not think of this as a silly exercise. It may be very important to you.

I am not assuming I have thought of all possible questions. If you can think of questions that are more meaningful for you, please use them. This is your exercise.

Although this book is primarily about changing careers, such a change may have a profound effect on other aspects of your life and the lives of those around you. Before identifying a new career area, let us examine the basis of your desire for change.

What Are The Things That You Like Best About Your Life?— Write down as many things as you can think of, include at least ten things.

When I was a little girl, like lots of other little girls of my generation, I read a book called *Pollyanna*. Pollyanna was a beautiful little girl who was quite poor and who had been taught by her missionary father to look for the good in every happening. It was symbolized by the fact that when a pair of crutches came in the missionary barrel instead of the doll she wanted so badly, she expressed her thankfulness that she did not need them. Our times have become so cynical that it is an insult to call someone a "Pollyanna."

While an attitude of sunshine and light is not very functional in present times, the cynical attitude which replaces it is not always very useful either. The good things in a person's life may have been adversely affected by change simply because they were not considered in the change process. You cannot change some things in your life without affecting everything else to some degree. Many people who have carried out substantial changes have found that while they did eliminate or improve some things they did not like, they also adversely affected something they did like. Don't neglect listing the good things in your life that are important to you and which you do not want changed.

What Are The Things You Like Least About Your Life?—You may want to write these down very privately. Even those who love you may react strangely if they see some of the things you write down. Be honest with yourself, considering a career change may be part of a larger picture.

What Things In Your Life Would You Change If You Could?— Athough this category seems strongly related to those in the previous item, they may not be identical. There may be changes that you would like to make that are not listed above. Also you may not want to change some of the things that you don't like about yourself. Although the latter may seem strange, psychologists will tell you that this is often the case. Which of these things are most likely to be able to be changed?

Who Are The People You Like Best Who Are Around You Now?—How will these people be affected by the changes you would like to make? Would the changes be good for them? If you do select a new career what will it mean to them? If you are considering different careers, what will the impact of each be on these individuals?

Why Do You Like These People?—In this regard, the question of the difference between like and love is often raised. There are those whom we love whom we may not like very much and there are those whom we like and admire whom we do not love. Think of the characteristics of those whom you like. Are there some characteristics which you wish you posessed? What are they? What could you do to develop these characteristics? How would this affect those whom you love? How would this affect your choice of a new career? Would these characteristics be important in the new career? This question may seem to be more related to changing your total life than an assessment of a new career but many times they are closely related.

Who Were The People You Have Liked In Former Years?—For many of us, life was different when we were young. We may have lived in a very different part of the country and have done different things. The people we knew then may be quite different and perhaps have different values than the people who surround us now. Is your desire for a change related to this? Who were the people whom you liked in years gone by? How do the values these people demonstrated relate to your own values and professional goals?

Why Did You Like These People?—This question follows the previous question with little need for explanation. Have you ever before considered what made you like, respect, and admire certain people? Stop and give it some thought.

What Characteristics Do You Like Best About Yourself?—This is an important question, remember that this is no time for false modesty. If you think that you are very intelligent, beautiful or friendly and this is important to you, admit it, at least to yourself. List at least ten things.

What Do You Like Least About Yourself?—This is equally important. Once more, list at least ten things. Remember, don't show your lists to anyone. You want to study your own feelings and attitudes and you must be clear about them. Many people will find this the most difficult assignment. We try to hide our weaknesses even from ourselves. It is a matter of our own survival. Some of the things you don't like about yourself may be causing you problems in your old work area and can obstruct you in your new career choice.

What Kind Of Jobs Have You Held In The Past?—Include everything, from your first job (paid or unpaid) to your present one. Don't forget to include volunteer or elected positions.

What Did You Like Best About Each Of These Jobs?—Once more include at least ten things about the jobs. Are some of these things the same for several jobs? Has some of your dissatisfaction with different jobs been repeated a number of times?

What Were The Things You Liked Least?—Again, be just as prolific in your list.

Have You Ever Been "Fired","Laid-Off" Or Almost Fired From a Position?—Have you ever admitted to yourself exactly what happened when you were terminated? Did the situation repeat itself? Why? You cannot always have had a boss "who was out to get you" or peers who were jealous. What elements are you putting into the situation? Are you repeating your failures without learning from them? Think about this very carefully. If you have a recurring problem in this area, you may need some counseling to clarify the situation.

Rank Your Jobs In Order From The Worst To The Best—Did some of the jobs which were at the top of the list have some of the same "best characteristics?" What were some of the common characteristics of the worst jobs? If you were to change jobs, are there some characteristics which you would like to add to the "best list?" Perhaps higher salary is one or more responsibility, more freedom, being your own boss, working outdoors, working with people, doing creative things ... these are only a few very basic things. What is one person's dream job is another person's nightmare. The important thing is to isolate some of the characteristics which are important to you. The next two items will help you refine some of the elements which either should be present or absent in a new career.

What Are Ten Characteristics You Would Like To Have Associated With Your New Career?—This is a very important list and will be used to a large extent in the next chapter.

What Are Ten Characteristics You Would Not Like To Have Associated With Your New Career?—This list is equally important. Remember that there is nothing magical about the number ten. You may have more or less than ten characteristics on your list if that is more comfortable for you. It is important however, to generate enough characteristics to make the exercise useful.

Now make a list of "Number One Dreams." This is an emotional get- away list. If you could do or be anything in the world, what would you choose? Put it on your list. Have you had any dreams in the past? Put them down. Remember that there are no constraints—not lack of time, talent, you are not too old or too clumsy nor do you have too many other responsibilities. You can be an astronaut, a ballet dancer, a doctor, a teacher, a judge, a movie star, a hero or heroine, a great artist, a writer, a bulldozer operator, a high wire walker, a sea captain. Anything goes on this list.

The next step is to survey this list of dreams and move onto another list those for which you have absolutely no talent or historic possibility of attaining. Do not move any for which you lack training or education. If you are changing careers, it is most probable that you will have to undergo some formal training in order to be prepared. Notice that I did not say eliminate them. I did not say cross them out or laugh at them. I said remove them. Call this list number two dreams.

Is there anything left on your list of number one dreams? If so you are lucky. Many people face a blank piece of paper at this point. You may think that what you have left on your list is exactly what you want but you owe it to yourself to research your new career a little more.

The next step is to supplement your lists. Begin with some of the topics you put on the second list. Are there some things on the list that, although impossible in themselves, might suggest some realistic goals to you?

For example, you may never be an astronaut, but is there some way you could work in the aerospace industry? Could you be a scientist or could you be a computer programmer for the National Aeronautics and Space Administration (NASA)? Could you begin as a secretary in an aerospace company that does aerospace work and develop some expertise? Could you move up in that company to a position of responsibility? Could you report on space and other science activities or could you be an artist who works for a publisher who does science fiction or hard science books? The network can go on and on. It will be different for each person but the process will be the same.

Your interests may be very different. You may never be a ballet dancer, for example, but is there some role you could have with a ballet company or with a civic cultural center which you might enjoy and to which you might bring some expertise and enthusiasm. These may be extreme ideas, but I think you understand what I mean. Add these related career possibilities to your list.

Now begin to add those activities that appeal to you and for which you may have more ability to achieve than the ones you eliminated from your original list. After you have written down all the things you can think of, you should turn to other sources for ideas.

Your next task will be finding out about opportunities that may not have existed a few years ago. There are many sources of ideas for new careers. Some may relate to the job you are presently performing, there may be a position in the same company which you may seek, or you may want to go to a totally new work area and or even geographical area.

Your public library or local high school may have a selection of materials on careers. College catalogues can also be a source of ideas. The *Dictionary of Occupational Titles* published by the U.S. Department of Labor lists thousands of jobs, most of which you probably have never even heard of. This book, which looks like a New York City phone book will be discussed in detail in the next chapter.

The Bureau of Labor Statistics publishes *Occupations in Demand*, a monthly newspaper which lists job titles, locations, salaries and phone numbers. It is available from the Consumer Information Center, Pueblo, Colorado 81009 and can be found in most libraries and at Job Service offices in every state. This will not only be a source of job listings for you but will also provide you with a general range of salary information and geographic location for certain positions.

The *Occupational Outlook Handbook* is published annually and may be obtained from the Bureau of Labor Statistics, Occupational Outlook Service, Washington, D.C. 20212. This book will give you not only information about specific careers but also some idea of the future of those careers themselves. It will be found in most libraries.

There are many sources of information about the types of positions which exist in your geographic area. Your local newspaper is always a good source. Also the local or state employment office may have a counseling center or at least a list of job openings. The personnel office of a company that interests you may also have job openings posted. Both of these will display salary and job qualifications while the newspapers often do not give this information. One of positions you see listed here may prove to be part of the "right" career ladder for you.

Do not limit yourself to old ideas and old concepts about careers. Recent advances in technology have opened up large numbers of career opportunities. Look for something new. Think big. Think of something that will be exciting to you.

Do not neglect opportunities with your current employer. Investigate all types of training programs with your company or with similar firms. Companies do not always expect you to be able to perform all aspects of a position when they hire you. You will have to demonstrate that you have the potential but companies may be willing to place you in a program to develop that potential.

I recently visited NASA, officially known as the Johnson Space Center, in Houston, Texas. The place is fascinating, of course, but it was made so much more so by a young lady who served as a tourguide. She had an incredible amount of knowledge about the history of the space program and the performance of the various crews. She could describe in detail the history and use of the different components of the vehicles on display there. Since this is an active center, she was asked questions about the projects people were working on as we passed or observed them from booths. She was able to give us some idea of the current projects at the center without going into extensive technical detail. I asked the young lady what she had done to prepare for this position. She told me she had been a secretary at the Johnson Space Center and had applied for the opening. NASA provided an excellent training program and she was always reading about the new developments to increase her knowledge.

This young woman had made a very distinct career change using an opportunity within her own company and a training program offered by them. She had the skills needed for the position. She was intellegent, interested in the space program, an excellent speaker, patient with questions and genuinely liked dealing with the people who came to NASA. An opportunity like this may not present itself to you, but do not neglect those that do come along.

Note that in the example above, I listed a few of the tourguide's characteristics that applied to her new job. If she were considering a career change, she might have made a list such as I have asked you to make. She would have included a great number of characteristics about herself and the kind of job she liked to do. Since she seemed to be such an organized, talented young lady, I can estimate that her skills as a secretary were good also. Let us examine some of the characteristics of the new position which might be positive. She met many people. She talked about the space program. She was viewed as a knowledgable person and respected by the individuals who came in contact with her. The subject about which she spoke was interesting and there were always new developments.

There were negative aspects to this position also. The Johnson Space Center is a very large complex and the displays are in many buildings. The tourguide is constantly on her feet, walking from one building to another with a large number of flights of stairs to be climbed on each tour. Some of this walking is between buildings that may not have been too pleasant during Texas's heatwave of 1980 or in rainstorms, etc. She has to dress well and there is a great deal of wear on her shoes. She has to always be ready to talk and answer questions. She has to always be prepared. Not all visitors are nice. Some may want to go into restricted areas and be difficult to control.

When this young lady listed the positive and negative aspects of this job, the positive must have won by a large margin since she took the position and seems to be very happy in it. Some of the things which I list as negative she and you may not view in that manner at all.

This is why it is important for each person to make their own list. I can tell you how to do it, but I cannot make the judgments for you as to what you like or do not like.

USING OUTSIDE HELP

You may have wondered why I have not discussed the possibility of paying an individual to do this kind of analysis for you. The reason is that I sincerely believe you should do it yourself and this book is intended to help you through that process. You can be instructed to really investigate your potential and you know that you really care about the results.

You may have seen advertisements encouraging you to visit a *career counselor.* This is one of the new careers that has developed over the past few years to assist people who are changing careers. The counselor is not responsible to help you find a new position and this fact is often not understood by the person who purchases the service. A good career counselor will take you through the same type of steps as this book. I recommend that you do this on your own unless you are very uncertain of yourself and your future. This is the case with many individuals. In some cases, the services of a career counselor are offered by an employer as part of termination.

In view of the complexity of modern life and the number of career changes one can anticipate going through in a lifetime, it would seem that this is a needed profession. The problem is that there is not a clearly defined body of knowledge which the counselor must have nor is there adequate licensing and consumer protection with regard to such positions.

Career counselors charge a fee and sometimes very large fees. The career counselor may or may not administer certain placement type tests and may or may not take you through the process we will be examining in this book. Some career counselors are excellent and will be a big help to you but others may do little more than talk to you about ideas you had when you entered their office. If you use a career counselor, use the same standards as you would apply to any other professional. Be certain that his or her reputation is excellent, know what the service is going to cost you, have an advance agreement as to what you will get for your money and remember that abilities are different for different individuals. Local licensing laws vary and you might want to check into the requirements which are in affect in your area. Since you will have made a good study of career change before you finish this book, perhaps this would be a good career for you.

If your current position and/or career has fallen victim to technological advances or some other factor you may be forced to find another career. Many companies are using the services of "outplacement" specialists. By outplacement is meant the process of letting someone be terminated while helping them to understand the reasons they were let go and to find a new direction for them to take in their career. The quality of outplacement firms varies. If your employer is offering this service, take advantage of it and participate fully in what it has to offer.

Remember that a career counselor or an outplacement specialist is not an employment agency and does not help you find a job. His or her role is to identify job areas which may be the "right" ones for you. I am not implying anything negative about career counseling agencies. They have a role to play and some are excellent but enter the process with caution and knowledge. I must admit that I personally believe in "do it yourself" when you can.

We also must consider employment agencies. Employment agencies are in the business of matching people up with jobs but for the most part these agencies work for the employer. If you are considering a career change, you may be seeking counseling from the employment agency when that is not its role. Some agencies charge a large fee to the person seeking the job while others have the fee paid by the prospective employer. If you become involved with an employment agency, check its professional credentials and determine just what you will get for your money. Whether you pay the fee or the employer pays, check on the contract you will sign. What if the job doesn't work out either from your point of view or from the employer's? Who pays the fee then? I had a friend who took a job that turned out to be terrible but she still had to pay the fee once she accepted the position. She couldn't quit that job until she got the fee paid off and it was a substantial amount of money. Be clear on all the rules before you sign the contract.

In addition to good advice and meaningful direction which can be obtained through personal contact and discussion, there also exists a number of tests, some of which must be administered by a psychologist, which can help you discover the right career for you.

The *Strong-Campbell Interest Inventory* is an example of a good test. It is one which has recently attempted to expand its data base to include women in many of the areas which were considered to be male dominated. I know this because I contributed to the data base on the interests of women Ph.D. Physicists. The Strong–Campbell test questions your interests in a seemingly endless number of areas, and then compares your profile with those of people who are already in those careers. It must be professionally scored.

The *16PF* gives you information on your personality traits many of which are directly related to your career choices. The 16PF and Strong–Campbell tests must be professionally scored.

The *Career Compatibility Profile* is a self-scoring counseling instrument that can be obtained from the Women's Center for Executive Development, 111 East Wacker, Suite 2210, Chicago, Illinois 60601.

You may find that some of these or other tests are given by the placement group at your college or even the counseling office of the local high school or vocational school. Inquire if you can take the test there, even if you must pay a fee. Many of the specific results are easily understood. You will only need to have the test administered and scored.

Self-assessment, counseling and testing can all give you information to answer that important question: What new career is the right one for you?

3

New careers

If someone asked you to write down the titles of all the jobs that exist you would have an impossible task. New jobs would be created as you were trying to list the old ones. Some of the jobs would become obsolete or radically different even as you were collecting information on them. Even if the search were limited to all jobs that you yourself could perform, the task would still be monumental because you would have to investigate the characteristics of a large number of jobs, some of which would be right for you and some of which would be quite wrong.

The good news is that you won't have to conduct this search. Uncle Sam has done for you and it probably is available in your library. The bad news is that there are 20,000 entries.

If you have already chosen a new career area, I congratulate you. That's wonderful, but I would still like you to go through the listings. Although you may be quite certain of your selection you will improve the odds for success in your career change if you do this review. Your selection may well stand up against all the other opportunities you review, increasing your certainty that you are doing the right thing.

If you are like most people and are uncertain about which career to choose, the review will be an absolute necessity. Your knowledge of job areas and career ladders is limited by your experiences. This listing will dramatically increase your knowledge of the world of work, as the high school counselors refer to it.

In order to develop a list of possible careers you will have to match your abilities, interests, likes, dislikes and limitations to the characteristics of a number of jobs. A number of characteristics accompany these listings.

The Department of Labor, during the 1930's, tried to organize the titles and characteristics of all the jobs that existed. They created a system of numbers that identified a number of characteristics associated with different jobs. Jobs that are somewhat related are classified together. This information was published in a large volume entitled the *Dictionary of Occupational Titles* This book is used by many, including the division of unemployment. It is available in almost all libraries and in such places as state unemployment bureaus. The *Dictionary* will be invaluable for you so discover a location where you can use one for an extended period of time. You certainly don't need to own one but you will need a number of hours with it and you may need to copy some pages. Bring some change with you for the copy machine.

The book has been updated a number of times. In the edition that was published in 1949, there were 17,500 entries. The 1960's represented a period when a number of new types of jobs were created by technology and there was a substantial increase in the number of entries. A substantial effort was made in the seventies to reduce the number of entries by eliminating those which are generally "out of date." The edition which was printed in 1977 contains approximately 20,000 jobs. The recent return to basic living and arts and crafts may require that some of these deleted entries be reinstated during the 1980's.

Considering the number of entries, the odds are in your favor that there is a position for you in the *Dictionary of Occupational Titles*. Since I have just told you the number of entries I can see you sitting there saying "She isn't going to ask me to read all of those entries and make lists from them, is she?"

Of course I am! You will have some other tasks to do first, however.

We are going to work together in a scientific fashion to select your new career. Even if you have already chosen a career, I recommend that you follow the steps outlined below. It will either confirm that you have selected the right career or it will inform you about other options.

The *Dictionary* has an excellent section in the front of the book which describes its use. In the back of the book is a small section which decribes some of the philosophy underlying the book. Before you can use it, you must relate this philosophy to your own life. Although the book is often used only to classify titles, the items include many pieces of information about each job.

Each job is classified using a coding system. The first digit for the general code number for the listing specifies the ocupational group. The third edition of the *D.O.T.* lists the following as the key to the first digit in the number.

0 Professional technical and managerial occupations
1 Professional technical and managerial occupations
2 Clerical and sales occupations
3 Service occupations
4 Farming, fishery, forestry and related occupations
5 Processing occupations
6 Machine trades occupations
7 Bench work occupations
8 Structural work occupations
9 Miscellaneous occupations

The nine groups are broken down into eighty-four, two-digit divisions and the divisions, in turn, are subdivided into 603 distinctive three-digit groups. These groups form the basis for the second and third number in the job number code.

The fourth, fifth and sixth numbers are somewhat subjective. As indicated in the fourth edition on page 1369, each job title is related to the degree in which the worker is expected to function in three areas: *data, people* and *things*. Only "occupationally significant" relationships are indicated, since every person, in every job must be able to function in a general manner to each of these areas.

These headings play such a significant role in the designation of the job title that they are represented by the fourth, fifth and sixth digits of the occupational code numbers. The highest value in each of the columns in table 1 is selected for representation in the job number.

DATA (4th digit)	PEOPLE (5th digit)	THINGS (6th digit)
0 Synthesizing	0 Mentoring	0 Setting-up
1 Coordinating	1 Negotiating	1 Precision Working
2 Analyzing	2 Instructing	2 Operating-Controling
3 Compiling	3 Supervising	3 Driving-Operating
4 Computing	4 Diverting	4 Manipulating
5 Copying	5 Persuading	5 Tending
6 Comparing	6 Speaking-Signaling	6 Feeding-Offbearing
	7 Serving	7 Handling
	8 Taking Instructions-Helping	

Before you can identify your standing on these characteristics, you must know what they mean. The definitions as used by the Department of Labor in their coding are given in the Appendix. The department's definitions may not be your definitions (or mine). They may not seem to be complete or may allow too much overlap. Whatever your judgment, these are the key to the numbers assigned various jobs and they will help you to identify the various components of positions so that you do not have to study the full 20,000 entries in the same detail.

The ratings from 0 to 6, 7 or 8 are not judgments of the value of the items. A job that involves a 0 to a much larger extent than any other number is not a better or a worse job, but a *different* job. The list has been arranged in order of complexity with the more complex component including the simpler elements. Please read and reread the explanation, if necessary.

If you have skipped over the pages which have been reprinted from the *Dictionary of Occupational Titles*, please go back and read them. If you find some of the phrasing difficult and/or unclear please reread those items.

We will use these definitions as a starting point for an analysis of your likes and dislikes with respect to job tasks. These, in turn, will form part of the basis for identifying the characteristics of a new career. The next step then will be the identification of the restrictions on the position. The final step will be selection of the career itself. Now, time to get out the paper and pencil again.

Almost all positions involve working with the three basic elements of *data*, *people* and *things* but most focus on one of these elements to a much larger degree, than the others. If you had to select one of these as the primary focus for your new position which would it be? Which characteristic would be second? Would it be a close second or would it miss by a great deal? Which one would be third? Would it be tolerable or would it be dreadful if the new position contained a great deal of that element? Some people hate working with numbers, other people love it. Some people do not like a great deal of interaction with people. Other people are afraid of or are repelled by machines. To each his or her own as long as each knows what that *own* is.

Remember this part of the analysis when you are selecting jobs to review in greater depth. The fourth digit of the code number for the job identifies the highest component of *data*. The fifth digit of the code number identifies the highest component of *people* and the sixth digit of the code number identifies the highest component of *things*. Look for those items which include the functions you like in the more complex form and the functions you don't like in the simplest form and with the least emphasis.

Notice as you study the definitions of the Worker Functions how they can vary within the same category. Under *people* you have a broad variety of choices. A 2 might be attached to a teaching type position while a 4 might go with an entertainment role and a 5 might accompany a salesperson's position. A person who would make an excellent teacher might be a terrible salesperson even though he or she would have to interact with people in each position. On the other hand, the same person might be good in all three roles but in most cases will prefer one of them.

Many positions are not completely clean with respect to the worker functions. You can translate that as "life is not simple." But the process still is valid and valuable. Write down the numbers under each of the digit headings which would interest you and write down those which would be a no-no. There is no point in looking at entries which would involve components which you couldn't stand.

After you have conducted this analysis, you are still faced with the prospect of going through the 20,000 entries. The task will be lightened, however, by the way in which the entries are grouped. Don't just plow into the book. Study the categories of entries, they are grouped together in very useful ways. For example, if you have always been interested in biology, you will find several very different types of positions under general headings that involve the word *biology*. The indexes offer different ways to find related entries. You will be able to eliminate many, many listings through their indexed heading by the code number or by the first few words of introduction.

A substantial amount of renumbering occurred from the third edition (1965) to the fourth edition. This is shown in the following list of examples of entries from the *Dictionary* Some of the titles were chosen to show you the variety of jobs which are classified. Study the examples before you begin your work so that you will have a good understanding of the design of the entries.

JOB TITLE	3rd edition	4th edition
Perfumer	022.181-014	022.161-018
Poising Inspector	715.387-022	715.384-018
Poet	130.088-022	130.067-042
Pocketed-spring inspector	780.887-046	780.684-050
Secretary	201.368-018	201.362-030
Seamstress	782.884-078	787.682-030
Teacher, nursery school	359.878-026	359.677-018
Teacher, art	149.028-010	149.021-010
Teacher, technical ed.	090.228-026	090.227-010
Telephone operator	235.862-026	235.662-022
Pony ride operator	349.228-010	349.224-010

Do you know what a poising inspector, inspects? There are many interesting listings in this book you can look up. Note how many of the rating numbers changed. Pay special attention to the fourth, fifth and sixth digits.

Bring filecards with you and jot down such information as code number, job title, pertinent characteristics and page number in the *D.O.T.* For those entries which seem to be most interesting, be a big spender and make a copy using the copy machine which can be found in most libraries. Bring change because they often do not have the facility for making change. Your time is more important than the little bit of money that is involved. After all, you are planning your future and you will want to study this information after you leave the place where you are studying the *D.O.T.*

What new ideas did you get from this book? Remember not to eliminate those ideas that really appeal to you but for which you do not have the training. We will address that topic later. Make these additions to your class one and class two lists of possible careers. Did you find a lot of new things to add to your lists? Were some of these jobs ones you did not think about before? Were some of these careers ones you had never even heard of before?

In spite of the fact that there are so many entries in the *D.O.T.*, there may be jobs that you have thought of but which have not been listed or which may not have been listed as being attractive. A number of entries considered to be outdated were removed in this edition and a substantial number of new entries took their place.

Some of these positions may not be out of date which respect to what you want to do. I haven't looked to see what the *D.O.T.* has to say about the manufacture of buggy whips but I would venture a guess that it is not listed anymore, if it ever was. Many careers which are related to the making of hand-made products are not necessarily out of date any more. Many crafts that were once considered to be only profitable in terms of pleasure are now producing good incomes for their practicioners. If your interests lie in this area however, you will probably not find these these listed in any general catalog, but you will have to look in specialized magazines to discover your opportunities. Add these things to your lists, if they interest you.

A number of career areas project an increase in positions in the next few years. The *Occupational Outlook Handbook* which is mentioned in the previous chapter not only discusses the new careers but also attempts to project the future of those careers.

The rapid rate of technological development and of increases in the standard of living have combined to create a large number of new positions. The development of the computer, alone, has created a long list of positions which did not exist to any large extent except in a few research laboratories even twenty-five years ago. With respect to computers, there are people who design them, make them, test them, program them, put groups of them together, run them, fix them, sell them and use them. These are only categories of computer related positions. Within those categories are a number of different types of positions. In addition, computers touch on a number of seemingly independent careers. Dress designing and pattern making, for example, rely heavily on computers these days.

Technology and increased services in the health-care field have combined to make it a very important area for new careers. Biomedical instrumentation has resulted in the development of amazing new instruments. Don't be frightened by the mention of medical technology, however. The gentle touch is still needed in the health-care field.

At times it seems everyone works for the government. Perhaps that will be true someday, because government employment has been determined to be on the rise. Not everyone sits at a desk and runs the bureauocracy. There are a number of very highly skilled positions opened in government work which are similar to those to be found in private industry.

Criminal justice is another area that has expanded rapidly. Bachelors and graduate level degree programs in criminal justice have changed the field to some degree and women as well as men are now selecting this area as a career.

Business is a complex area and there are many opportunities for those who are contemplating a career change. I have known a number of former teachers, for example, who have gone into the area of training and the development of training materials. The areas were related in a very broad sense but not in a specific sense. The former teachers needed some training themselves before they could make the change.

If you have identified a general area that interests you, search the magazines or journals which are written for people who work or study in that career area, for the types of positions available. Positions which are available are often advertised in those magazines. You may not always get a lead as to the salary offered for a career which seems interesting, but you can trace that down even if you have to answer an ad.

If your town is small, there may not be a great variety of careers or jobs listed in your local paper. However, it is possible to get a copy of the *New York Times* as well as some other newspapers in many libraries. The *New York Times*, Sunday edition, like a number of other newspapers, has a section which lists a number of career-related positions in display ads as well as a section which has small classified ads. You may find a number of interesting positions advertised here which are interesting and which you may never have thought of before. Add those to your list which seem interesting.

You yourself may know of positions which are too new to have been included in the books and magazines which you have read or the general areas I have suggested above. Add them to your list as well.

On the next pages, I have compiled a number of positions which I have found listed in the classified sections of newspapers and in magazines and journals. These are but a small section from the types of positions being advertised in a number of geographic locations during 1981. You might find some listings of interest to you on these pages. There may be titles which you need to investigate in the D.O.T. or with a career counselor.

Review your newspapers and college catalogs. Investigate interesting job titles and continue to add to your lists.

Hopefully, you will now have a pair of long lists to work with. Remember, the number one list is for special jobs and dreams. The number two list is for those occupations which didn't make it to the number one list but still have some appeal for you.

CAREER LIST

The careers listed here are given in no particular order. Some are well known and well established and others are new. Perhaps there is something here which you can add to your own list.

SCIENTIST
TEACHER
DOCTOR
BANKER
CREDIT MANAGER
QUALITY CONTROL SUPERVISOR
PRODUCTION SUPERVISOR
MANAGER
PERSONNEL COORDINATOR
RESPIRATORY THERAPY TECHNICIAN
X-RAY TECHNOLOGIST
MEDICAL TRANSCRIBER
PHYSICAL THERAPIST
PATIENT EDUCATION COORDINATOR
LABORATORY PHLEBOTOMIST
SYSTEMS PROGRAMMERS
GRAPHIC DISPLAY PROGRAMMERS
AERODYNAMIC and PROPULSION ENGINEERS
MICROPROCESSOR SYSTEMS ENGINEERS

PROGRAM MANAGERS
INSTRUCTORS IN TECHNOLOGICAL AREAS
PROJECT ADMINISTRATORS
ANALOG/DIGITAL ENGINEERS
PRODUCTION PLANNER
MECHANICAL DESIGN ENGINEERS
COMPUTER OPERATOR
RECREATION DIRECTOR
CITY PLANNER
ARCHITECTURAL DRAFTER
PRE-SCHOOL TEACHER
INTERIOR DESIGNER
DANCE INSTRUCTOR
PROGRAMMERS
TRAINING DIRECTOR
SURVEYOR
CARDIOLOGIST
ACCOUNTANT
FIELD SERVICE ENGINEER
LAWYER
INVENTORY CONTROL ENGINEER
PASTE-UP ARTIST
PHOTOGRAPHER
ADMINISTRATIVE ASSISTANT
FIELD SERVICE ENGINEER
PHARMACIST
OPTOMETRIST
TRAVEL AGENT
RESTAURANT MANAGEMENT
HOTEL MANAGEMENT
REAL ESTATE MANAGEMENT
ENVIRONMENTAL ENGINEER
DESIGN DRAFTER
ACTUARY
COMPTROLLER
WRITER
CONTRACT ADMINISTRATOR
PUBLIC RELATIONS
JOURNALIST

ADVERTISING
PURCHASING AGENT
LABOR RELATIONS
SYSTEM RESEARCH
MARKETING
ELECTRONIC TECHNOLOGIST

Following are ads that appeared in a recent Sunday paper.

Test Engineer—Experienced engineer to engage in long-term test equipment design and build program. Practical experience is a must in the design and fabrication of digital/analog test equipment. Experience with PCB test equipment is also helpful. This position requires a degree with a minimum of three years experience.

Park Manager—Graduate of accredited college with bachelor's degree in recreation administration or related field. Possession of degree in recreation administration or related field may be substituted for (1) year of required experience. Possess minimum (4) years responsible supervisory park management.

Technical Instructors—Seeking professional instructors to instruct on installation and maintenance of Mitel's KPABX Systems. Trade school/industrial qualified telephone equipment instructor, telephone equipment installers or maintenance personnel preferred. Academic qualified teachers may be considered.

Talented Writer—Your gift is needed for this public relations firm writing features and news stories.

Data Entry—Expanding corporation has need for data entry operators. Will accept experienced or will train good typist who would like to break into the data processing field. Pay commensurate with ability. Can lead to computor operator supervisor position for the right person.

Chief Flight Instructor—Local FAA approved flight school needs qualified chief flight instructor.

Paste-up Artist—To lay out newletters and prepare charts for stock market advisory service.

Operating Funds Analyst—Bachelor's degree with a major in accounting, business or public administration and at least 2 yrs. auditing exp. either in private industry, public administration or public accounting. A master's degree in business or having successfully passed the CPA examination will substitute for 1 yr. of required work experience.

Personal Trust Administrator—Opportunity to join a winning team of results-oriented professionals in one of the fastest growing trust departments in the area. The ideal candidate will possess an undergraduate degree and a minimum of two years experience in all phases of personal trust account administration. If you are looking for a career position offering competitive pay, excellent benefits and exceptional growth opportunity send your résumé to...

Scientific Programmer—This candidate will analyze scientific applications software written for CDD 3400 in Fortran IV, additional duties will be to design, code and document software for SEl 32/55.

Material Control Coordinator—This candidate will direct and supervise the accounting, requisitioning and expenditures of all material and supplies required for the project, several years experience in military supply or industry which deals with the military is required.

Technical Wirter—Technical writers entry level and experienced to participate in the documentation of a new product. Knowledge of computer systems necessary.

Biologist—Assist in research on biological controls of aquatic weeds. Duties would include field and lab work, with aquatic insects and fauna, M.S. with major course in one of biological sciences or BS + 1 yr. biological work experience required.

Executive Director—of community-based organization call...

Systems Programmer (to $30,500 per year)—Requires college degree in computer science and four (4) years experience in system's analysis, system and maintenance.

Pre-school Teacher—Needed to assist director and teach part-time.

Senior Auditor—we are currently seeking an individual interested in upward mobility and an opportunity to join a professional team involved in financial and operational audits. Qualifications include 3 to 5 years audit experience CPA, CIA or advanced degree and supervisory experience is helpful but not required.

4

New schemes
old dreams

Ridicule can be more effective than any knife to slice apart a dream. Have you ever had that happen to you? Have you ever given up on a dream because of what others said about it? Are there any old dreams left on any of your lists of possible careers? Are there any survivers of sharp-tongued ridicule? Keep them—nurture them—they may not be impossible to achieve. They will have to be studied and protected until you are able to defend them.

There are many individuals who have had the courage and made the opportunity to follow a dream at a career change point in their lives. We will discuss some ways to accomplish this and look at some individuals who did this later in this chapter. First, we have to find the right career for you. It may be that old dream and then again, it may not.

You want to make a change in your life. Do you want to make a change for the sake of change or is the selection of a new career very important to you? There is nothing wrong with wanting some change and selecting your career to be the focus of this change. In this case, however, you must realize the change in career may not bring about the change in your life which you desire. Study the question of change very carefully. How much can you expect from this change?

You cannot consider a career change in isolation. Your career takes up a large part of your life.

Let us assume you have twenty-five years left of career productivity and let us assume you work an eight hour day. Executives work more like a sixty-hour week than a forty-hour week but we'll settle for the lower figure. Now let us assume you get five weeks of vacation and assorted holidays. That means you will be working 25 x 47 x40 = 7,000 hours. That is a long time to be unhappy in a job. Remember that just changing jobs may not solve your problem if it is not initially job related.

If you are certain that you want a new career, you must then consider all the steps involved in the change as very important to you. Every step is part of the link in the chain. There are not too many shortcuts. Attaining a new career will not be simple. It will demand a great deal from you and from your family. You must be certain that the new career is the right thing for you.

How do we find the right one? Back to the lists!

You have racked your brain, probed your soul, analyzed a book with 20,000 entries and who knows what else. The product of all your work is hopefully a list or lists of careers that appeal to you.

Now that you have created all of these lists what do you do with them? Why, you break them up into smaller lists! You now have a number of career areas on at least two different lists. Make each of these careers titles the heading of a new page.

Under each career heading list

1. Your abilities which support that career area. Include potential that could be developed through training or education.
2. The characteristics associated with the career that match either items on the " good job characteristics" list you made before or are positive ones that you can identify from reading about the career or talking with someone who is already in that position.
3. The characteristics of the career that are on the "bad job characteristics" list you made before or which might seem to be bad. Again, the fruits of your research.
4. The things you would have to do in order to prepare for that job. Include, for example, going back to school, moving, borrowing money to study or start a business.
5. The anticipated reaction of those whom you care about to this career.
6. An estimate of the odds on your getting a job in that career field at your age and with your talents. This is perhaps the most difficult

factor to project, but you must do it realistically. You may need to talk to someone in this field in order to make a realistic appraisal of your future in this field.

7. A complete description of what the job is really like. In order to do this you will have to talk to people who have that job. Although it is sometimes difficult to find people in a particular career in your geographic area, it is important to find out just what a job is really like. What appears to be a glamorous occupation as described in a pamphlet, may really have some aspects which will not appeal to you at all. What are the day-to-day tasks? What are the opportunities for advancement? Find out before you make the change. You may have to do your searching for answers by telephone if you cannot accomplish this in person.

8. List the beginning salary for this career. What kind of increases could you expect? How long would it take to move up in this field? Note that I inquired about the starting salary. You may be able to get more than the starting salary because of your past experience but don't depend on it. Inflation has done strange things with salaries. Beginning salaries have had to be raised to keep up with inflation but longevity increases don't even seem to be keeping up with beginning salaries and non-relevant experience is not always considered in placing you on the salary scale. Can you live on this income? Is it better or worse than what you have available to you now? If you have to make a financial investment will you be getting a good return on your money? Is this an important consideration for you?

9. You may be suffering from boredom at the present time? Are there repetitive elements to the new job?

10. Indicate the kind of feelings the new career will cause you to have. Pride, excitement ... what will these things be? Will you increase your positive feelings toward yourself? Will others?

11. Would you estimate that changing to this career would accomplish for you some of the things that are important for you?

12. Put in the answers to any other questions which you have identified as important but which I have not included above. Do this kind of evaluation for all the careers that you have written down.

Are there any careers that you can definitely eliminate at this point? Do not use the criteria of education or cost as a basis for elimination but you may use the other criteria.

Now we are going to play a "number game" with the careers which remain. You do not need to follow the results of this game. The choice of a new career is too important for that but the analysis you will have to do to get your numbers will reveal a number of things to you.

The results of this will give you some insight into your true feelings. You may need a calculator to carry this out. It is a little program which I call "Decision Assist."

DECISION ASSIST

STEP 1   Identify the careers which you are evaluating. Include your current career. Write them down using a single word identifier that will bring the concept of the career clearly to your mind. You may have as many careers included as you wish.

STEP 2   Identify the characteristics of the new career which would be important to you. Express these characteristics in one or two word phrases. Include all of the characteristics that are important to you.

STEP 3   On a scale of 1 to 10 choose a weighing factor for each of the characteristics. You may want to select the characteristic that is most important and give it a 10 or you may not. You can give the same weighing factor to more than one characteristic. For example two characteristics could be a 9. You can give decimal weighing factors to characteristics, for example you could use a 7.5 as a weighing factor.

STEP 4   Now you need to take a large piece of paper and make some columns. You will need a column for the characteristics and a column for the weighing factors. You will need two columns for each of the careers. For the mathematically minded, if N is the number of careers you have you will need $2 \times N + 2$ columns. For example, if the number of careers you are evaluating is 7, you would need $2 \times 7 + 2 = 16$ columns. Make your chart large. Tape some pieces of paper together if necessary.

The number of rows you will need is calculated differently. You will need a row for the headings, a row for every characteristic and a row for the total. If C is the number of characteristics, then the total of rows is $C + 2$.

Now put the headings over the columns. Over the first column put the word *characteristics*, over the second column put the words *weighing factor*, over the next *two* columns put the first career word, over the next *two* columns put the second career word, etc.

In the first column under the heading *characteristics*, list the characteristics on each of the rows. In the second column, under the heading *weighing factor*, write in the weighing factor you selected for each characteristic. Now you are ready to begin evaluating the careers.

STEP 5 Consider the first career with respect to the first characteristic. In your judgment, how does it do on it on a scale from 1 to 10? Write that down on the first row in the first column under that career heading. For example, suppose the first characteristic you have written down is pay and suppose you gave that characteristic a weighing factor of 8. Suppose the first career you think about is Computer Programming. Ask yourself how computer programming rates with regard to pay. Perhaps you give it an 8.5. Put a 8.5 down in the first column under Computer Programming and in the row marked Pay.

Now comes the step that has been known to be confusing to some people. If you don't understand exactly what I am doing, don't worry about it. Once you follow the steps in the example you will understand it. Multiply the score for the career on that characteristic by the weighing factor for *that* characteristic. This is the weighing factor written at the beginning of that row. Put your answer in the second column under the career.

Now go down to the next row and take a look at the second characteristic. Give the career a score on the second characteristic. Put the answer in the first column for the career and in the row headed by the characteristic. Multiply the score by the weighing factor for *that* characteristic. It is the weighing factor in that row. Put that answer in the second column under that career heading.

Continue to fill in all the numbers for the characteristics for that career and then move to the next careers.

STEP 6 Under each career, add up the numbers in the second column. These were the numbers that resulted when you multiplied the weighing factor by the score of each career on each characteristic. Put the totals in the second column under each career.

STEP 7 Compare your answers for the totals. Put the careers in order according to the totals. Do you agree with your results?

Decision Assist Example for Career Selection

Henry Jones (or Henrietta) has an Associate degree from a community college. He is presently employed as a construction worker. He is considering changing. He has identified that he is good at mathematics and is willing to go back to school in order to be prepared to enter a new career.

Henry has identified the following career areas as being interesting to him, including his present one: construction, electronic technology, computer programming, computer operator, purchasing, accounting, automotive factory work. These become the headings for columns in the chart below.

The characteristics of the job that are important to him have been identified (in any order) as pay, geographic location, security, repetitious, fringe benefits, more education, creating things, future advancement, pride. These are the headings for the rows. See the chart below.

The entries under weighing factor were decided by Henry (or Henrietta) on the basis of only his own feelings rather than any outside influences. *Pay* and *Future* are important. If a career demanded a great deal more education, Henry saw that as negative as gave it a small number. Someone else might have given it a large number.

Take a look at Table 4.1 for Henry Jones' first Decision Chart.

TABLE 4.1 DECISION CHART #1 FOR HENRY JONES

CHAR.	W.F.	CONS.	E.T.	C.P.	C.O.	PUR.	ACCT.	A.F.W.
PAY	8							
GEO.	5							
SEC.	8							
REP.	4							
F.B.	6							
M.E.	3							
CREAT.	7							
F.A.	7							
P.	6.5							

BECAUSE OF THE SPACING OF THE PAGE, ABBREVIATIONS HAVE BEEN USED ABOVE CORRESPONDING TO THE CHARACTERISTICS AND CAREERS DISCUSSED.

If Henry now begins the next step (Step 5), he will have to decide how construction ranks on each of the characteristics. You can see how he ranked things in Table 4.2.

Table 4.2 DECISION CHART #2 FOR HENRY JONES

CHAR.	W.F.	CONS.	E.T.	C.P.	C.O.	PUR.	ACCT.	A.F.W.
PAY	8	8						
GEO.	5	6						
SEC.	8	8						
REP.	4	4						
F.B.	6	3						
M.E.	3	0						
CREAT.	7	5						
F.A.	7	1						
P.	6.5	4						

In order to obtain the value for the second column under the first career you have to multiply the value in the first column under the career by the weighing factor for that row. You can then add the second column to get a total value for Henry's choices.

Table 4.3 DECISION CHART #3 FOR HENRY JONES

CHAR.	W.F.	CONS.		E.T.	C.P.	C.O.	PUR.	ACCT.	A.F.W.
PAY	8	8	64						
GEO.	5	6	30						
SEC.	8	8	64						
REP.	4	4	16						
F.B.	6	3	18						
M.E.	3	0	0						
CREAT.	7	5	35						
F.A.	7	1	7						
P.	6.5	4	26						

The total for *construction* would be 260. Remember that the values of these numbers are entirely Henry's. Someone else may have had a higher or a lower value for each of the items. Henry would then complete his chart and put the careers in numerical order.

Try it with a small number of careers at first, until you get used to the process. By the way, this technique can be used with a number of decisions you have to make. Try it with choosing vacations. If you find it terribly confusing or if math is a large problem for you, skip this exercise. It is a useful one however.

This process is really a simplified version of a more complicated decision program and is not fail-safe. It has some flaws but the alternative requires some very high-powered mathematics. This process is really fairly straightforward and serves to give you another instrument, a very subjective instrument, to use in your selection of a career. Try this with your items. How does it come out? Do you object to the result? If so, then you have some conscious or unconscious bias toward the items on your list. That is good. It is good to have such feelings. At the least, the calculations will cause you to react negatively toward some items on your list and positively toward other.

The calculations give you yet another list, one that ranks careers in order of their performance in the "Decision Assist" calculation described above. Use this list to further refine your choices.

Take all of yours sheets now and once more make a list of the careers that are left. This will be your last working list unless you have now crossed everything out and have to start over!

Now that you have all these lists, what do you do? At some point you have to stop making lists and choose! The choice will be easier if you can project some plans for attaining your goal. Please, please don't scrap those old dreams.

Changing careers, going back to school and following dreams both old and new have become more readily acceptable in recent years. I have only to look around me to give you some examples of people doing this very thing. If anyone feels that I am telling their story, I probably am (and I am very proud of you.)

An engineer I know entered medical school in his early forties, at considerable sacrifice to himself and his family. He is an excellent doctor in a large city and has long ago demonstrated just what a good idea this was.

A young black woman who had a fifteen-year career in art management (museums, galleries) also went to medical school. This had been an early dream of hers but she was discouraged in her dream by high school guidance counselors. She went to medical school with the emotional and finanacial support of her family and today has a successful practice.

An airline pilot with a number of auxiliary interests, began to paint somewhat late in his very active working life and found he had tremendous talent and a growing market. He has phased in this new career on a gradual basis and is now making a very fine living from it. He also derives a great deal of pleasure from his new occupation which will carry him through what would normally be his retirement years. Again he has a wonderful, supportive wife who has helped him along the way.

A teacher I know became a successful textbook author. Not only is he an extremely wealthy man as a result, but he has done a great deal to make a difficult subject interesting and to humanize the curriculum in his field. He never thought that this would happen when he spent those long hours writing that first book after school was over for the day.

Family support was obvious in the case of the wife of a prominent local man. Her enrollment in law school was followed closely by that of two of her children. All three have had a successful experience. Mother and son are already practicing and daughter will graduate next June.

A gentleman who has reached the limits of opportunity within industry because of the lack of a degree has returned to school to get a degree in electrical engineering on a part-time basis. His son is enrolled in a similar program in another school.

A widow with ten children, some of them grown, who had worked as a teacher aide for a number of years, returned to school and obtained her own teaching degree.

A teacher who began taking singing lessons as courses toward the renewal of her teaching certificate was encouraged by her teacher after only a year of lessons to enter a competetion against people who had been studying for years. She won and thus began a second career of opera singer in addition to her regular teaching position. This year she will have an opportunity to sing in an opera with Pavarotti!

Another teacher who went to a community college for a degree in mortuary science found that he could complete the program in a year because of his previous work. He now carries out this second occupation on the weekends and is on call at a number of funeral homes for emergency replacement of their regualar staff.

A woman who was tired of office work opened a consignment shop for children's clothes.

Not everything has gone perfectly for everyone. Some succeed, some fail. Those that tried, however, at least followed their dreams and that was important to them.

The family plays an important positive role in many of the successful cases. It is not only a matter of the family allowing you to change your career. It is a matter of the family participating in that career change.

If you are going to build the scheme for moving to the new career, you will have to take the following steps.

1. Identify the new career which you would like to enter.
2. Research all aspects of this career.
3. Identify your strengths and weaknesses with respect to this career.
4. Involve your family in the process of considering the new career. You may want to involve them in the process earlier than this.
5. Obtain the additional education needed to enter the new field if necessary.
6. Prepare the image necessary for you to enter the new career.
7. DO IT.

Always keep this new goal in proper perspective. Your career is part of your life, an important part, indeed, but still only part.

The "scheme" is very straightforward. If the new career seems to be the right one for you, taking everything into account, then you must make the necessary sacrifices to do it.

You will have to make plans, work hard, sacrifice perhaps, take chances, do what you must do to obtain it.

5

Change is a family affair

For many people the key to the selection of a new career and the successful pursuit of that goal lies with the family. Family support can help make a dream come true while family opposition can all but destroy the dream. The young person making his or her first career choice is generally influenced by parents, older siblings, possibly other family members and teachers. There may be some person in the family who acts as a role model. While the young person may or may not be generally independent of the family unit, the level of responsibility for these people will be very small.

The person who makes a mid-life career change often has a wife or husband and children to think about and to consult with. His or her range of responsibilities is more extensive. The older person who is single and who is responsible for himself is also by no means free of stress in this consideration. This person will have to "make a living" for himself and it may be more difficult for him to change without the support of a family.

One may be legally free, an individual and liberated, but one's life and happiness still depends to a great extent on one's family.

You may have noticed that I did not include the family in the very first step of your career change planning, which was described in the last chapter. Some people may be able to involve some family members from the very first, but most people have to do much of the self-exploration on their own. They need to formulate a tentative plan before exposing their ideas and themselves.

We began the last chapter discussing how ridicule can destroy dreams. Dreams are fragile. They must have some shape and form before you can reveal them. You must first establish confidence in your dream before you discuss it with a great number of people.

There are some questions which you must answer to your own satisfaction before you reveal your plans. Who are the people in your family whose opinions are most important to you? Whose are least important to you? Who are the people in your family who will be most strongly effected by your change in career? Who will react most strongly, either positively or negatively, to your announcement? There may be very little overlap in your three lists, but there will be some people on each list who will have an important effect on your decision. For example, the change may effect your children greatly, but if they are very young, you would not be affected by their opinion. If they are older, they might have a great deal to contribute to your decision. You may have a brother-in-law who is negative about everything you do but he would not affect you directly. He might influence someone who would affect you, however, like your husband or wife.

A coach studies his opponents very carefully. I do not mean to imply that members of your family are your opponents but you must be concerned with the dynamics of the interaction. Remember the stress chart that was discussed previously. You need to minimize the stress in your life if you are going to make this change a successful one. You need to list the major individuals with whom you will have to interact on this matter. Which of them will influence your decision? To whom are you simply making the announcement?

Think about these individuals carefully. What kind of a reaction do you think they will have with regard to this change? You are part of your family and your family is part of you. For some of you there may be tension already present in the family unit, which may be a source of some of your desire for change. Changing to a new career will temporarily add to the stress in the family unit although ultimately it may relieve some of the problems.

What made you begin to think about changing your career? Was the original desire to change your career *yours*? It may have been initiated by another person such as your wife or husband. It may be someone else who feels that the change is necessary. There may be desires for more income, less absence from home, more future, more stability or more pride. These desires may be expressed openly or they may be presented very subtlely. Given the dynamics of American society, this situation is true more often for men than for women.

Women are more likely to be personally unhappy with their present career or lack of it and come to the conclusion that they must change rather than to be *pushed* into this by another. Even if you feel you are being give a slight shove in this direction, the decision to change may indeed be the correct one. Sometimes others know what is good for us before we ourselves ascertain it.

Be clear in your own mind about your family's feelings before you present your ideas to them. Everyone in your family is an individual, just as you are. Don't think of them as *them*. Think of each one as a person whose help you will need to make the choice and to make the transition. Those whom you know will never help you at least can usually be persuaded to make little trouble if it is handled correctly.

Your family is important to you and you are important to them. Any change you make in your life will affect your family and they may be frightened by the idea of change. They may feel insecure. They may not understand your level of unrest or boredom with your present position. Inadequate salary or opportunity for advancement are easy to explain but many sources of dissatisfaction with a position have much more subtle causes. These are often difficult to explain. They are also difficult for someone who does not actually do your daily work tasks to understand. Try to work out some ways of explaining to them just why you are reluctant to stay with your present work or career and need to move to the new one.

A woman who desires a career may have a difficult time explaining her dissatisfaction with her present life to her husband. She may want to expand herself and gain some of the respect of the community through her new career. Her husband may believe that this desire reflects some inadequacy on his part or some ingratitude on hers. These feelings must be understood, but ultimately the person changing his or her career must decide what is best. Understand the motives behind some of the reactions you will get.

The decision to change your lifestyle and career will ultimately be yours but do give some attention to what your family and friends tell you. It is possible that they are more correct than you are willing to admit with respect to your choice of career. While they may have other motives, which they don't even realize, they may also be correct in what they are saying. Try to give an unbiased review to their ideas. They may know you at least as well as you know yourself.

Understanding is the key word in getting your family to be on your side. Remember that there may be a delayed reaction of your family to the suggested change. It may take a while for their reactions to really develop, either in a positive or in a negative manner.

At first some families will be neutral if not positive. As the change begins to take place, the family member may become concerned and express dissatisfaction with the concept of changing careers. This reaction may have its source in fear and that fear itself may have many sources.

Family members may fear that you will fail in this career change and that certain things, such as income, will be worse than they were before. Another fear is that you will succeed in the change and that this success will leave no room in your life for that person. He or she may feel that you will not need that person as much any more. This is a common fear of husbands whose wives enter an exciting career which makes them independent. Another emotion related to the career change of a family member is jealousy. Family members may be jealous not only of your success, but even of your ability to change some part of your life. They may not want to deprive you of this pleasure but simply desire it for themselves. They may be in as much need of change as you are. The fact that they are not able to improve their own situation has been accentuated by your change.

Others will find that you have less interest in them because of your interest in your new career. You may have less time to spend with them. You may have less money to spend on recreational activities. These may, indeed, be facts not just illusions. You will have to be sensitive to all possible reactions. Some of them may surprise you.

Do not forget that a negative reaction on the part of someone may be the *RIGHT* reaction. It is possible that what you have chosen is not the right choice. It might be right for you and not right for your family. It might not be right for anyone.

I'm not sure how Gauguin's lifestyle change could be assessed. It probably was good for him, but not good for his family. No one interviewed him about that later in life, I suppose.

Any change will certainly be easier if you have your family on your side. You will have a better opportunity to do this if you are clear about your reasons for change, if you involve your family in the decision-making process and if you plan this change taking their feelings and needs into account.

If your career change is going to require preparation such as returning to school, the situation will be further intensified. You will be taking time and money away from the family unit in order to prepare for your change and may encounter resistance. You may find it difficult to get the privacy to do the studying or preparation that you need for the new career. Some of the tasks that you have been doing may have to be taken over by others and there will be understandable resistance to this. The expenditure of both time and money will have to be planned for carefully.

Time, unlike money, is a difficult quantity to borrow. Your family needs you. If you have children they will only be young once. If you borrow too much time from the family unit it will have a negative effect on everyone's life. It is important to be aware of this and to make accomodations for it in your time plan.

The question of time management and planning will be addressed in an another chapter but it has a substantial impact on your familiy's response.

Don't be surprised by negative reactions on the part of family members and friends...or even by the butcher, the dentist or your favorite bartender. Everybody believes that they are entitled to an opinion.

Don't feel that your family does not love you if they are resistant either as individuals or as a family unit. They have their problems too. Be sensitive to them. Their love for you may be the very source of their negative reaction.

Before you present your plan, your dream, to even your closest loved one, be certain of what you really want to get from this change. You must be able to express clearly your reasons for change. You must be able to describe what is wrong with your present job or career path. You must also have a good understanding of the new career or careers you are considering.

You should never give your family the impression that you made up your mind without talking to them, even if this is the case. That seems like a deceptive thing to say, but even if you are convinced you are making the right choice, you must give your family the opportunity to give you their ideas.

Unless you are used to family gatherings, it is better not to present your ideas in a group format.

You may want to begin by talking with someone in your family unit who will be supportive. You are looking for creative ideas for your own future. Even after reading the 20,000 entries in the D.O.T. you may still have passed over the position that is just right for you.

Evaluate the situation. What is it that each member of your family will be most concerned with? Some may be jealous or fear your success. Some may fear you will not have time for them. Some may fear you will move away. This is a fear which will occur with those who will move with you and those who will stay behind. Some may fear that there will be less money or that their life will change substantially. Evaluate these potential charges. Is there any truth in them? Are there ways in which you can minimize the negative effects of the change on others?

For some this will be a very important consideration since they are anxious to sustain their family unit. Others may not even make this gesture since they consciously or unconsciously desire the separation of the family situation.

If there is already trouble in the family, this element of change may be sufficient to cause the final break. Be aware of this. Again the question, what do you really want from this change? Is the career change important or is it a tool to effect a more substantial change in your life? This may be a good change. There are many single people who still live at home and who work in a family business who are unhappy. They might become new people—happy people—if they could find the career they really wanted all the time and pursue it. A new career could mean a whole new life for them.

Friends can be as much of a help or a hinderance as family. If you have close friends, they may be part of your extended family in influence if not in responsibility. Be cautious of negative comments from your friends. They may have your best interest at heart. They may be right. They may also be jealous. If the new career may seem to give you greater importance or financial reward they may have sub-conscious feelings against it. They may feel the work you must do will take you away from the time you can spend with them. Be cautious of possible ridicule from this area. If you want to retain these friends, ignore their negative reactions to your decision. Understand their motives, they may not be aware of them, themselves.

If you have a good family unit and if you want them to be on your side you can accomplish this through patience and understanding on your part. Listen to them. They may be right. They know you and love you. Make them listen to you. Plan to include them. Think of the problems which might occur because of the career change and try to minimize them through understanding and planning.

6

Putting off until tomorrow what you can

Procrastination is not a four letter word if you count the letters, but the puritan work ethic which still affects our lives to some degree has made it one. It is a word that in fact has had a negative effect on our creativity both as individuals and as a nation.

Idle hands are the devil's workshop.

Don't put off until tomorrow what you can do today.

The real truth is that if you don't procrastinate about the right things at the appropriate time, you will never have time to do some really important things. If you don't learn to do some selective putting off until tomorrow, tomorrow will be just as dull as today. On the other hand, if you procrastinate about the wrong things, tomorrow and the day after will be even duller. The difficult thing is to decide what are the really important things. *Important to whom* is perhaps the key question.

Many individuals who would like to change their careers or some other part of their lives find themselves caught in a set of repetitious details and convince themselves that they haven't got time to make the preparations to accomplish their goal. There is always time. It is just a matter of finding it. Sometimes this means putting certain things off until tomorrow.

I am asked, over and over, how do I do it all? The answer is that I don't do it all, all of the time. I do enough of everything some of the time so that everything seems to be done most of the time and there is no revolution. Is that clear? Probably not, but a little confusion makes for an interesting day. If you keep everything too clear and in too rigid a pattern, everyone will notice if you don't get something done.

If I had not put off a few things, and more than a few things over the years, I would not have written this book or any number of other things I have written. I would have not painted any pictures or taken any photographs because all of these things were, in a sense, speculative. These were not things I had to do as part of my responsibilities. They were things I liked to do. They are not in the same class as doing the wash and scrubbing the floor or the oven. I do not like to wash or scrub floors although I do like the resultant cleanliness. I don't even like to *talk* about cleaning the oven, although I do love to cook. I do like to write and paint. Many would have considered these an absolute waste of my time. Neither of these things were guaranteed sources of income. If they had been it might have give them some justification under the puritanical code. They were, however, important to me. Somehow I managed to keep my family in clean clothes and the house relatively straightened up while doing the things which I considered more important. I have posted a little hand-painted ceramic magnet on my refrigerator door which I bought at a county fair in New England last summer. I'm certain that heads must have turned as I bought the piece because I was laughing so hard. The inscription so completely describes the way I work at times. It says, "If it weren't for the last minute, a lot of things wouldn't get done."

I'm afraid that is true at times. It isn't always a matter of procrastination, however. It is a matter of becoming comfortable with planning things and planning them right down to the wire.

It is amazing how much time you cannot actually account for in your day. If only we could get back some of those idly spent hours back. The next section will discuss the management of your time and the way to squeeze a little extra from each day. If you are going to actually accomplish the career change you have selected, you will have to begin putting some things off until tomorrow so that you can work on other things today.

Identify the things you must change in yourself and start a personal program for them. Do they involve physical fitness, grooming, new clothes, improving your speech and/or grammar? What program can you get started to improve these things? Riding your bicycle before dinner, jogging before breakfast, a set of grammar lessons on tape that can be played in the car to and from your present job? What will you put off to do these things, a few minutes sleep, or listening to your favorite radio station. See what you can squeeze in if you think about it!

Identify the educational training you must obtain in order to prepare for your new career. Map a schedule to obtain this training. Do you need refresher courses, or are you starting from the beginning in your program? How long will it take you? Where can you get the program you need? Don't procrastinate with respect to finding out these details. Put yourself on a schedule. You may have to put some other things off until tomorrow but they will be worth it.

Do you have a résumé to write and a set of inquiry letters to type? Get that rough draft finished. Have a friend review it for you. Find a good typist if your own fingers can't reproduce the necessary flawless quality which is needed.

Do not, however, put off spending time with your family. Your children will only be young once and that time can never be reclaimed. You will also have to be conscious of the needs of your spouse or other family members. Involve them in what you are doing. You want to minimize any negative feelings which they will have about the career change. They may fear that the new career will take you away from them. Don't begin by taking your time from them.

The things you decide to put off should be explained to your family and close friends if they are affected in some manner. Perhaps you will have to hire someone to do some of the jobs which you are going to have to postpone in order to reach your new goal. This might be a wise investment of both time and money.

Remember that procrastination can be a good thing if it is handled and does not just happen. The key to everything is the management of your time.

Equality is a word for our own century. No one in days gone by thought or dreamed of equality. They may have wanted to have as much money or success as someone else, or they may have wanted to be free, in terms of the horrible specter of slavery. They may have wanted to be as beautiful or as loved as someone else. In many parts of our own world the word *equality* has no more real meaning than it did in America in years gone by.

We cannot legislate equality except for equality under the law, which is, of course, important. Every person is an individual. We differ in size, in color, in sex, in intellegence, in wealth, in talent, in power, in beauty. The list could go on forever, it seems. These things cannot be made equal in any two individuals. Not only are there the natural limitations, there is also the lack of a standard. For example, the concept of beauty differs not only with culture and background, but also with personal taste.

The only real equality is the equality of time.

Every person—rich, poor, brillant, insane, beautiful, ugly, happy, sad— has the same amount of time in a day. The length of our lives may vary, but in each day we have the same amount of time.

The question of time management is a serious one in the industrial setting. There are a number of time-management workshops devoted to this. High-level executives must organize their time so that their company gets the maximum benefit from their activities. Before a plan can be developed, the executive, often in cooperation with a time management expert, analyzes the activities that take up his day. Things like phone calls and answering the mail are closely documented on a worksheet. After a clear picture of the range of daily activities is documented, a plan for managing that time better is created. Together we will carry out a similar study on the ways you spend your time and create a personal time-management plan for you. This will include time for you to work on things that you must do to provide for a career change while still maintaining your current position and life commitments.

I always remember the movie "Cheaper by the Dozen" when I think of time management. The movie, a charming family comedy, was made from the autobiography of the same title written by Frank Gilbreth, Jr. the eldest son of the twelve children of Frank and Lillian Gilbreth. These two individuals are often credited with initiating the concept of time and motion studies and time management. The movie and book contain delightful scenes of the father studying the children's pattern of brushing teeth, taking baths and dressing. The mother, a very warm individual with certain burdens as the mother of twelve children, took the father's place when he died suddenly on the way to present his theories at a European conference. In days long before women's lib, she became an important figure in the develoment of modern theories of business. The analysis of your daily life according to time spent may seem as foolish as the analysis of the brushing of the Gilbreth children's teeth. Please be certain that it is not. Time is even worse than money. You definitely can only spend time once and you can never get it back. We must make certain that those things which are really important to you are included in your time program along with those things which you are obligated to do.

The very first question to be answered is "What do you do with your day?" If I ask you this question, you will probably be able to tell me what has happened to large blocks of your time. You drove to work, ate lunch, went to a meeting, and cooked dinner. You may be surprised to discover how much time you cannot account for. It may add up to a considerable percentage of your day. If you do this analysis, don't show it to your boss. He or she may not realize how much time you are not able to account for. Because you cannot account for it does not mean that you are wasting the time. It really means that the manner in which the time was spent was not important to you.

The secret of time management is to spend your time more effectively, that is, to spend more of your time on things that are important.

In order to manage your time, you will first have to do a study of where it is going. Now for a long range assigment. Get a notebook which you can keep rather inconspicuously in your pocket or handbag and jot down all the waking hours in a day and what you do for those hours. If your days seem to be pretty much alike then do it for two weekdays and both weekend days. If they are different, do it for a little longer.

It may be obvious to you when you write down your time expenditure just where you can pick up a little more time. Or you may be frightened by the number of things you manage to accomplish in a day.

Next, set aside time allotments for the tasks which you need to perform.

The things you need to accomplish to prepare yourself for the new career may be single task items. You have to read through books on different careers. You have to spend time on the D.O.T., you have to develop a résumé or inquiry letters. Break these tasks down into small pieces and estimate the time you would need to accomplish them.

"I don't really have time to do these things," you might be telling yourself. Do you have fifteen minutes a day to spend? What can you do in fifteen minutes, you will surely be asking? For example, fifteen minutes would not be sufficient time to get anything accomplished in the reference section of the library, especially if you had to spend some time getting there. It might take you that long just to get the material you need from the closed shelves. If you drove fairly close to the library and stopped on your way home from work, fifteen minutes might be enough time to select some books on careers you are considering and check them out. You might get a great deal of information out of one of those books in fifteen minutes of concentrated reading. It might also be enough time to call a local school or college and find out what programs they might offer in a field you are considering. It might be enough time to work on one section of your résumé. It might be enough time to type a brief inquiry letter or prepare several envelopes. It would be sufficient time to study the classified ads in most newspapers. Papers like the *New York Times* always take a little longer but they offer so much more. Fifteen minutes of exercise or attention to grooming could fulfill some part of a personal appearance development program which you work out for yourself. You might be surprised at what you could do with fifteen minutes if you deliberately set aside that time to work on a specific project every day.

Many of the things which you will want to accomplish cannot be done in such short time periods, I realize. They can, however, be completed in reasonably small units. You say that it will take you four years to complete your degree. But that will not mean every single minute for four years. How many courses and how many hours per session and how many sessions per week will be the questions which you will have to answer. How many hours of homework for each hour of class will you have to spend on the average? Knowing this, you will be able to make a plan or schedule for yourself.

How do you schedule an evening class into your life? You just do, that's all. Don't expect it to just happen, you have to make plans for it. You may have to temporarily eliminate something else. It may be that you will have to postpone bowling, *Monday Night Football* or watching an evening soap opera. Something may have to go in order to give you enough available time to get something done. The thing you must do is to estbalish priorities in your life. Priorities don't exist in the same order for ever. If the important thing for you is to change your career you have to overlay the time expenditure for that against the things you do every day.

Make your immediate time plan and, if necessary a long range time plan as well. Evaluate your daily expenditures of time, fitting new items in and postponing others. Are there some things you enjoy doing that must be postponed?

Do you drag out things which you do not want to do so that they take up all your available time? Many people who are caught in this don't realize that they are doing it. Pretend you are working for yourself. Think of a task which you don't like to do. Would you pay yourself to do that task? Would you pay yourself for the number of minutes or hours it took you to do it? Or you would have fired yourself for being too slow? This is a way in which you can check up on yourself. Are you spending too much of that valuable time on tasks which you could be doing in significantly less time? Is one of the reasons, the fact that you are not being paid for this time? You may not cheat on your boss's time in the same fashion as you are cheating on yourself. The reason...your boss is paying you. The solution...pay yourself. Reward yourself with the time saved. Do something you like to do in the time saved. Who wants to rush scrubbing the floor if your reward is having the time to clean the oven. Reward yourself with the time saved by doing something you like to do. You won't be doing any less than if you had to spend the whole time doing the floor. Don't get caught in the puritanical loop of feeling guilty because you are not working. That is why you initially began to drag out the work. Once you find that you are able to get your tasks done in a more reasonable amount of time, you can begin to direct the time you saved in a way which will be directed toward your advancement in the new career.

While you are rearranging your schedule, don't eliminate everything you enjoy because that will depress you too much. Changing your career is a stressful activity and you will need to have some relaxation still left in your life. Are there patterns which you have established which need to be broken? Are you living in a rut? Study your expenditure of time and work your way out of the rut. Prudent procrastination may be the answer.

7

Catching up with time

Perhaps the most devastating discovery for a person who is changing to a new career is that time does not stand still for him or her. Although it seems rather arrogant to express the expectation in those terms, and few will do so explicitly, many individuals seem to expect this to be the case. It is most dramatically seen in the case of those who have not worked for a number of years. This is particularly true for women who have good educations. They return to the work force after a number of years of absence and expect to be paid as though they had been working and gaining experience during the intervening years. The person who has been working in another area expects to be paid for the experience he/she has gained in this other area. Neither of them may have experience in the area which is their new career. This presents a severe problem for the person who is going to hire them as well as for themselves. It is a very bitter adjustment to realize that the years which have passed may not be counted toward seniority in the new position. The situation is very difficult to face. The solution lies in compromise, maximization and adjustment.

It is important that the person entering a new career be aware of the pressures on the person who hires him or her. This will minimize potential bitter feelings. Cost-of-living raises have been competing with entering wages in many areas in such a manner that new employees are sometimes paid almost the same as people who have been in the field for a while. To the new person entering the field this may not seem true but it is in many cases. This arouses bitterness in some individuals who have been working within a field for a number of years. Inflation is destroying not only our ability to buy but our ability to gain some kind of credit for our work performance.

The person entering a new career must make every effort to gain maximum credit for his or her past experiences. They must face the factor of time very consciously.

There are some negative aspects to time. Time has made us grow older. In a world that puts Youth on a pedestal, we may feel less attractive than when we were younger although it is possible for us to actually be more attractive. The person who is changing careers must present an attractive image. Image is more than appearance, although, the way you look is, of course, a part of your image.

Time should have made us wiser. Yet many people may be out of date in a particular field or with respect to a particular skill. There will be a need to evaluate required skills or preparation. Although not all fields have changed drastically, no field has stood still in the past few years. If you were trained for a specific career, you will have to assess where you stand with respect to current knowledge and present practice in your chosen field. You will also have to discover a way for yourself to upgrade your skills or learn new ones. How can you demonstrate your abilities? How can you convince a prospective employer that you are capable in the new career?

Time should have made us more secure in our interactions with other individuals. When entering a new career, however, an individual may feel like a young person taking his or her first job. How can you gain new poise and security? How can one show confidence which one may not necessarily feel? How can one translate skills learned in a previous job into a new work area? How can you work with people who may be much younger than you are?

How can you work *FOR* someone who is much younger than you are? This is a question you will have to face in advance of the change. Although you will certainly try to maximize your opportunities, you may indeed find yourself reporting to a younger person. You had better be aware of this beforehand. Time did not stand still for you, but the intervening years did not count for as much as you may have estimated. This may take a severe adjustment on your part. It may be necessary for you to accept it, at least on a temporary basis. Do not be ashamed. It does not represent failure on your part. It is a fact of life. It is is a result of the fact that time did not stand still.

How can you evaluate where you stand with respect to the new career? How can you boost your starting place on the career ladder? How can you turn back the clock? How can you make time stand still? You can't but you can try to compensate for it.

Self-evaluation is always difficult. Some individuals are able to objectively review themselves, but they are very few in number. Many people have managed to become immune to their faults and to cover up their weaknesses. These individuals have a far more difficult time in setting their skills in proper perspective. They find themselves possessing the attitude "why don't they realize how wonderful I am?"

Few people will realize how wonderful you are. You will have to convince them with your performance. Unfortunately, life is not always fair and the talents of many people are not recognized. If you are going to make up the lost years, you will have to carefully plan the steps needed to reach the next position on your chosen career ladder.

Other sections of this book will discuss creating your image and improving your skills. Here we will discuss abstracting the characteristics of your present career and life that will support your new career.

Take a piece of paper and rule off a number of columns and rows. Place the name of the positions in the first few steps of your new chosen career over the first few columns. Place the names of other jobs you have held or volunteer activites you have directed and your educational experiences over the other columns. Under the new career columns list the characteristics associated with your new area. Under the other headings list the characteristics which were associated with your other positions. Under education list those things you have learned that will support the new position.

Are there things under the other columns which will support the new career? Are there items which you can use as evidence that you have done things similar to those required by the new career?

The more items you can find to support the new career, the better evidence you have that you should not have to start on the first rung of the new ladder. The better chance you will have of starting at a more advanced position and of actually being able to perform the tasks required of the new positon.

What you must do is develop the concept of *transfer of training* with respect to your new career. In simple terms, the transfer concept states that one has learned specific ways of performing in one position which can be carried over (transferred) to another position. When you do this analysis, the kind of things that have been transferred will be clearer to you. You are trying to convince your prospective employer and perhaps yourself that you have actual experience in certain areas because of characteristics of work you have done in the past.

If your experiences are limited, or if you have not worked in a while, you may find yourself stretching the point a little, but this is still a valuable exercise. You will use the information you develop in both writing your résumé and in your interviews. You may also use it to convince yourself that you do indeed have some preparation for the new position. If you are able to identify a substantial amount of support, this evaluation will help you gain new confidence. If you cannot find many similarities, you will have to realize that indeed you will have to start pretty close to the bottom in the new area.

In order to do this evaluation effectively, you will have to thoroughly study the new career and, in particular, the entry level positions in that career. What will you have to do or know in the first job you get in this career ladder? What would be the characteristics of the second position, the third, etc.?

If you have problems identifying types of characteristics, take a look at the headings in the *D.O.T.* Remember the book with the 20,000 job entries? Remember all those headings and characteristics associated with different jobs? Remember working with people, places and things? You have thought about the characteristics of the new career. Have you thought about the characteristics of your old jobs? They don't even have to be charactersitics which you particularly liked. You are trying to build up a portfolio of supportive experiences.

If you have not worked for a long time you will have to pull together some of the characteristics of the volunteer activities in which you have engaged. Stretch your ideas, but don't get ridiculous. Driving the children to baseball practice does not necessarilly prepare you to be a director of transportation. Running a major charity drive does give you excellent experience in organizing details and managing people.

Remember, the person who hires you will have to answer to someone else and explain why he or she though you were qualified for the new position.

Let us suppose you have done your homework. You have related your past experiences to the demands of the new job. You have improved your skills in the new area, you have worked on your image and done all the things you need to do. You will still have to adjust yourself to the fact that unless something extraordinary happens you will not be given full credit for all your working years. This is especially the case for years for which you have not worked for a salary. No one could ever convince me that staying home to raise a family is not work, but many people regard it in that way. Although homemaking is definitely work, it may be that there are not many characteristics associated with it that can be transferred to the new career area and represented as countable experience. Many women who have had good educations, worked for a few years and then dropped out to take care of their families, are very resentful when they are placed in an entry level career position. If you have done everything you can think of to maximize your position, you may have to adjust your thinking. You may have to accept the role of beginner—once more.

If you are not able to turn back the clock and make up all those years at the beginning of the new career, it is possible that you will be able to move more quickly in the new position than a younger person. Beginning in the right place is important but so is getting promoted. You will have to show your new employer that those past years were not wasted and that you have the skills needed to move you along at a faster rate than your younger colleagues.

Identify the reasons that people get promoted within your new career position. What are the characteristics needed for the next promotion? Would more education be of assistance? Do you dress, act and perform as though you are in the next position already? Reinforcing your own belief in yourself, will help you to catch up with time.

8

Sidelines

For those who are not able to commit themselves to a career change the option of a sideline is often a viable alternative.

It would seem that moonlight and dreams go together, and in many cases they do. This may be especially true with respect to a new career. *Moonlighting* is the name often given to the activity of those who supplement their regular work with additional employment in an area which may be different from their main position. A second job may be the answer to your new career dilemmas.

You may choose a new career area for a number of reasons. One reason for the choice may be that the area will give you greater financial security than the previously held career. At times a person may really be selecting a career, as as opposed to a job, for the first time in his or her life. Many times the career the person dreams of entering is one in which it is difficult to get a position. It may be that the person could get a position in the new field but could not make an adequate living.

I would love to write or paint for a living but it would be many years before I could even begin to generate an income from that activity which is equal to that which I earn in my present position. It would be a risk for me to give up my regular position and write full time although to date, my writing has been successful. In addition, I like my present position. Until I feel that the time is right, I will "moonlight" and continue to write after work and on the weekends.

My friend the pilot, who is now a successful painter on a full time basis, maintained his other position and painted part time until his talent developed and his income rose to a sufficient level to support him. He no longer flies now, except for pleasure, and is able to paint and teach painting full time.

Another friend of mine who is a teacher is also a part-time mortician. He is keeping the security he has as a teacher while building a second career. He hopes that when he retires from teaching he will be able to open his own funeral home and is already working toward obtaining that license.

A policeman I know who needed the security of a regular position to support his large family, does fine cabinetry work and remodeling of kitchens on weekends in the small town in which he lives.

A number of people work as consultants in a specific field while retaining their original positions. Some people have an excellent second career already established when they take early retirements from their first careers. This is important for those who may receive a pension after fifteen or twenty years of work in a specific area.

Individuals who retire from the military services often find themselves in the position of needing to develop a second career area. Some service areas provide an excellent preparation for a career in the business world. Some military and private sector areas are almost identical and full credit for experience may be given. Other areas, however, are quite unique to the service and the person seeking the second career may have trouble identifying transfer possibilities. The service offers many opportunities for schooling and some prepare themselves for retirement while still in uniform. They too, may begin to follow some career as something of a hobby while still in the service.

Those who are working in a technical field or a vocation may want to teach in that field. This isn't as simple a matter as it may at first appear. In order to teach in public schools in most states you have to have a teaching license. To obtain this license you must complete specific courses as well as a practice teaching program during which time you teach under the supervision of a licensed teacher. Most schools will not allow you to come into their program for only a few courses and the practice teaching. You may find that you have to take an extensive program in order to be permitted to practice teach. The rules are somewhat different for one to get licenced to teach in vocational schools but they still require some preparation on your part. Having a license to teach in one state does not mean you can automatically obtain a license in another state. These will all be things you will have to look into with specific regard to the rules for the community in which you desire to teach.

Teaching, however, is a career which can be done on a part-time basis. Many vocational schools have evening programs that require teachers who are experienced in a particular field. You might also try getting a license that allows you to substitute in a school. This means you would fill in for a teacher who is out for a specific time. Substitute teaching could give you an opportunity to discover if you would like to teach before you have made a full commitment to it.

Another place you can teach is in adult education programs. If you fear you might not be able to handle the discipline problems within a regular school, you would do well to consider adult education. In some ways it requires more patience than teaching in the regular program. The students vary more in background and even in ability. They are all there of their own free will, however, and that does seem to make the classes easier.

The pay for both substitute teaching and the teaching of adult education classes is not as high as that for teaching a regular day but it would give you an opportunity to test your interests and develop your ability. Teaching is one area where, except for vocational programs, little credit is given to you for work out of the field. You salary will depend, for most programs, on your teaching experience.

Some second career areas really relate to old dreams. A friend of mine (I'll tell you that she has a son twenty years old just to give you an idea of her age) has just developed a night club act with another woman. Both of these woman have other lives but they have put together a funny act and are doing on the weekends what they wished they had been doing all of their lives. Doing it on the condominium circuit, they will never get rich, but it has brought some satisfaction and excitement to their lives.

A young man I know who works in a resturant three nights a week is a dancer and a choreographer during the day. He hopes that someday he will be able to make a living in his profession of dancing. He is not involved in a career change but he is having to make do with a job until he can exist on the career he really desires.

I know several who have gone into the ministry as a second career. Some of these people were not able to enter this on a full-time basis at first. They obtained their training and began serving on a part-time basis.

The ministry seems to be an area a number of successful people are entering. Some have unusual backgrounds. One extremely successful minister with an extensive parish and television ministry, was a dance teacher before he decided to change his career. Many remember the beginnings of the little parish he started and which has grown so extraordinarily over the years.

Everyone has dreams, but not everyone is able to follow them on a full-time basis. Some people are moving into the second career because they were not able to follow their original dreams years ago. Others are only discovering their new careers now.

The creative arts are the most difficult to pursue whether as a first or a second career. The reason it is more difficult to switch to this later in life is that it no longer is so much fun to starve in an attic when you are making a switch.

If you are involved in an art or a craft, you may find yourself working on a part-time basis. You can make your items during the week, in the evenings perhaps, and sell them at various arts and crafts fairs on the weekend. Many people enjoy selling at the fairs and you will soon build up a following. I always remember an artist who had been a postal worker but enjoyed painting. As a lark, he took some of his work to a local show one weekend and sold the pieces for far more than he had earned that week. He began to paint more pictures using a particular style which seemed to be attractive to his customers. He continued to sell more and gradually began to go to shows farther from his home and to raise the price of his work. Eventually he quit his regular job and spent his full time painting and selling.

Some people do not like to try and sell their own products. It is possible for them to sell through specialty shops and through direct orders placed in response to advertisements in crafts magazines. There are a number of books which list sources for craft sales. The magazines in the particular speciality are probably the best source of the names of outlets for these products.

The Internal Revenue Service, which seems to dominate so many things we do, has some specific guidelines on hobby and craft sidelines which you might like to review.

Although professional artists are somewhat depreciating of the "Sunday painter" the same does not apply to writers. Very few writers are able to pursue that art as a full-time career. Writing, however, lends itself to being both a second career and a sideline. It does not take much preparation to write. You can jot down the exact phrase you need for the opening sentence of your work on the back of a napkin at lunch or on the flap of an old envelope. Much of writing is thinking...and rewriting. Don't be afraid that someone will laugh at you if you begin to write. Writing can bring you great satisfaction of itself, getting something published is a wonderful feeling.

Another benefit to beginning a second career as a sideline is that you develop a record of experience in the new career area. You will now have something to fill in on your résumé in that field. The experience may help you make up some of the lost time in the new area. It may help you begin at a higher than entry level position.

If you are trying to decide whether or not to pursue a second career and have some reservations about giving up your present position, try to think of a way you could do it on a part-time basis. Beginning your second career as a sideline may give you confidence in your ability to perform in the new career area.

Besides income, there are many benefits to entering the new career field slowly through a second job or sideline. It certainly is not possible in every field, but it occurs more often than you might suspect.

9

Creating the new image

I have a wonderful great-aunt who is ninety-seven years old. The difference in our ages is such that I can only remember her as "old". She has never considered herself to be old. When she reached her eighties she would joke about approaching middle age. Her mind is bright and her memory good. Her body, though aging, thankfully keeps supporting her.

We had a talk the other day about the person inside the body.

"You know," I said, "I don't feel any older than when I was in high school. I forget sometimes until I look in a mirror." She smiled at me. "I know how you feel," she said. "I don't believe it either. I don't know how I got to be so old. I don't even realize it until I pass a mirror. I look in and say to myself, who is that old lady there? Where did she come from, and then I realize it is me. I never thought I would be so old. I never feel I am so old."

We smiled together each knowing what the other meant—feeling the same although separated by a lifetime of years.

Do you recognize the face in the mirror? Does the image others have of you resemble the image you have of yourself? If you are going to change your career, possibly your lifestyle, and maybe even your whole life you may want to create a new image for yourself. You will certainly have to consider your images and evaluate them. Notice that I said "images".

An image may be defined as a mental picture. There are many images of *YOU*...Do you know what they are? Whether you want to create a new image or are happy with the old, you will have to examine these images from different points of view. At the very least, you must consider your own view, that of those who know you and the view of those who are just meeting you.

Because this book is for both men and women, you might think I would have to write a separate section for each sex. After all, men are not interested in advice on the length of a skirt nor are women concerned with the pattern of a tie. This is not the case, however. The question of image is so much larger than the details of skirt length and tie pattern that there is no need to distinguish according to sex. It may even be useful to know some of the things that must be considered by individuals of the opposite sex when they are creating their own images. Your image is a creation linking many components. One of them is your physical appearance.

PHYSICAL CHARACTERISTICS

First, let us consider your physical appearance. Included in this is the question of your physical health, your physical well-being and your physical characteristics. How would others describe your physical characteristics? How do you describe yourself?

We have all had to fill in those questions on applications about sex and height and weight, color of hair and eyes, etc. These answers are part of your physical image. Age and possibly race may be asked on some forms although there are times when employers are restricted by law from asking such questions.

Think a moment about these physical characteristics. Remember, I do not mean appearance now. That will be our next discussion.

Let's get out the pencil and paper again and write down the answers to some questions.

AGE
HEIGHT

WEIGHT
COLOR OF HAIR
RACE
WAIST MEASUREMENT
HIP MEASUREMENT
CHEST (BUST) MEASUREMENT

Don't feel silly. You don't have to let anyone see you doing this and you can burn your answers if you are afraid someone might find them in the wastebasket.

How did you answer these questions? What did you write down for your age? What is your birth date? Subtract your birth date from today's date. Did you write down the right age for yourself? If you are young, or old, you probably did. If you are somewhere in the middle you may not have written the correct figure. I must admit I sometimes have trouble myself unless I do a little subtraction. If you do not want to think of yourself as being your correct age, how old do you want others to think you are? Is this realistic? If you are forty, no one is going to think you are twenty. You might try for thirty-five, if that is important to you. The same may be even more true if you are older.

What did you write down for your weight? Go into the bathroom and get on the scale. You can take your shoes off if it will make you feel better. Is there more than a five pound difference between what you wrote down and what the scale revealed? Think about this.

You may be the correct weight for your age and height, or you may be too thin or too heavy. All scales may be your enemies but it is important that you be aware of your weight. I am not suggesting that you change your weight. I am only requiring that you be aware of yourself.

The current American fad is to be thin and this is reflected in those proper weight scales you find in diet books. What do you think your weight should be? It will vary according to your age. Does the chart you are using take age and sex into consideration? How close are you to the correct weight for your age and height? If you are very far off, are you content with your weight? If you want to change your weight, is there some realistic intermediate goal that you could set? If you are thinking of going on a diet, you should discuss it first with your doctor.

Now I want you to get out the measurement tape and check your body dimensions. Are you close to what you wrote down? In addition to the waist measurement, men should measure about one inch above the belt. Are you still quoting that old waist measurement for your waist and thinking that you are just as you were when you were in college when you are really hanging over your belt?

Do these measurements please you? Are there changes you would like to make?

You have written down some values, discovered the true values and made some estimates of what you would really like these figures to be. It is important that you once more be realistic. If you are no longer young, you should not select figures for your goals that are appropriate for a teenager. Try and work out a set of figures for yourself that would be right for you.

You may want to think about some kind of exercise program for yourself. Not only might this improve your measurements, but it might be very good for your general health and energy level. Again you should be certain to check with your physician before beginning such a program. The same exercise is not right for everyone. What kind of exercise can you fit into your lifestyle? Begin slowly and gradually increase your commitment to exercise.

What changes would you like to make in the characteristics you wrote down? I would like to be taller than my height of five feet, but I cannot do much about that. I would like to be younger, but alas that's out of my hands, although I must admit I've considered touching up those strands of silver among the brown. Perhaps I should. If the number of diets printed in the monthly magazines means anything, I am not alone in my desire to be thinner. Although that always seems to elude me, I am still working on that phase of my image. Is there anything about your physical characteristics that you would like to change?

Health is a factor that must be given strong attention when one is considering a change in career and possible change in lifestyle. If you remember the Holmes-Rahe Scale which appeared in the first chapter, considerable stress is encountered for a number of reasons when such a change takes place. I have already indicated that you should consult your doctor if you are going to go on a diet. If you are going to be able to physically survive, I recommend that you have a good physical checkup before beginning any major program of change. You may first want to give yourself a kind of mental once over.

Do you have any health problems that you have been neglecting or ignoring? Are you feeling good or are you dragged out? Do you experience shortness of breath or extreme weariness at times? How is your vision, your hearing? Depression can have serious effects on your health and you may have experienced some sense of "the blues" lately. If you have some doubts about anything, have a complete checkup. You should also try and be aware of your health as you go through this process. You may experience some changes in your health—for better or worse. Be aware of these changes and respond with good sense.

Your health is often shown through some of your physical characteristics. The shine (or dullness) of your hair, the expression in your eyes and the tone of your skin can all reflect your state of health.

Posture is extremely important. Although poor posture may only be the result of bad habits, it also may keep you from being admitted to the executive class. Posture is not fatal but it does detract from the image. It makes you look sloppy.

Many top executives, both men and women, carry out a regular program of physical fitness. This has several effects. People who exercise regularly find that they feel better. Exercise is good for them physically, it improves their appearance, and it gives them something to talk about at lunch.

Think about some of your other physical habits. I happen to think that smoking, for example, is bad for you and bad for those around you. If you smoke, how compulsive a habit is it? Might it keep you from getting a certain position? What do you look like when you smoke?

Do you drink much? Think about this honestly. Does it affect your appearance? Is it affecting you health or family relationships? Drugs, like alcohol, are a destructive component of many lives. You may instantly say that you don't take drugs, but consider those drugs prescribed by your physician. Do you, for example, take tranquilizers or sleeping pills? There have been a number of articles written lately concerning drug habits which began with physcian prescribed medications. Betty Ford, the former first lady, made some courageous and revealing statements about this problem that have caused a number of doctors and patients to re-evaluate their medications. Be aware of yourself. Do your best to take care of your health.

I do not mean, in any way, to discourage anyone who has a health problem or a physical handicap from considering making a career change. It is certainly as important to you and as possible for you as it is for anyone else. You are probably aware of the status of your health and will work with that factor in setting your new goals.

What I am trying to say is that health is very important and many people are not aware of the dynamic role that health plays in any kind of change.

Others, both those who know you well and those who are just meeting you, may be more aware of your physical characteristics than you are. After all, you don't go around looking at yourself all the time.

Note that although I am making a distinction between your physical characteristics and your appearance, they are related to some degree.

YOUR APPEARANCE

How do you appear to yourself? How do you appear to others? What do you see when you look in the mirror? What do others see? There are many components to a person's appearance. Such things as dress, hair, shoes, makeup (in the case of women) and accessories are all contributing factors to appearance. These can be carefully calculated to make certain impressions. Other factors such as speech, posture and personal habits, also make significant contributions to the overall impression you are making. These elements are more difficult to change and will require that you work out a program for changing yourself. Let us look at each of these quantities individually.

Dress

Clothes make the man (or woman), as they say. Although some people claim they do not have the time, money or interest to dress in a certain way, they cannot deny that clothes are a very large part of their appearance and play a role in creating an impression.

Thomas Watson, the founder of IBM, was very much aware of this factor and set criteria for the attire of his salesman that are still a standard in the industry.

You should dress not for the job you have, but for the job you want to have. That is a useful goal to keep before you especially if you are entering a new career.

Your clothes are an important part of your image. A number of recent books have focused on attire for the executive woman and/or the executive man. *The Woman's Dress For Success Book* by John T. Molloy, (Warner Books, 1976), which became a best seller, used a scientific approach to discover the type of clothes that would be most successful for the career woman. He found that the most successful *uniform* would be a skirted suit and blouse. The suit would be most effective in a color such as medium blue, gray, camel, beige, black or brown, and should be worn with a contrasting blouse. Black was somewhat inhibiting. I found the book interesting, did some adjustment in my own wardrobe and began make observations at professional meetings. I found that others had begun to read books such as these and that that number included the buyers in the department stores. I was suddenly able to purchase suitable clothing without having to go to very exclusive stores. One store I frequent now has a corner for executive women which carries some appropriate fashions. There was indeed a new preponderance of suits at the meetings I attended and the women wearing them looked professional. I might note that there is a wave of resistance to wearing suits and the "everyone-now-looks-alike" syndrome. Although there is no law that you have to wear a suit or dress, conservatively it is safe. If you feel confident, then you can vary your wardrobe considerably. A safe rule of thumb is that you should stand out only for the attractiveness of your clothing rather than the extremeness unless you are in either the fashion or the theatre industry.

Molloy's book for women has been matched by a number of books for men which help them learn how to dress in their quest for success.

The directions for men are similar to those for women if you replace the words "skirted suit" with the word *suit*. Conservative colors and cuts are always the best choice. You should be in fashion and fashionable without being guilty of following the latest fad. Loud plaids and checks are generally frowned upon, as are loud ties or socks. Individuality has its place, but conservative colors are safe. Again, dress for the job you want to have.

Women in particular have to be aware of the role they are seeking to play. If you want to be a business executive, then you should not dress in a fashion designed to highlight you as a sex object.

This does not mean that you should not try to be attractive. If you study successful people you will find they are generally very attractive. They may not be naturally pretty or handsome but they have a certain quality about themselves that is *quietly* pleasing. Note the word *quietly*. Loud clothes, on men or women is generally not the road to success. Clothes should be coordinated in color and in style. Although some designers mix colors and patterns that do not usually seem to go together, you must remember they are doing it for an effect. Sometimes this is so that they will be noticed. You, as a professional, do not want to be noticed for unusual, clashing outfits.

The cost of clothing is a serious consideration, but there are many ways around this. Your clothes should never look as though they came from the discount store. This does not mean that they don't come from such a store, it just means that they shouldn't look it. There are several criteria to use. Some of these will change with the years, but in general they remain effective. Good tailoring is important in clothing for both men and women. If there are threads hanging from seams and shoulders or collars don't fit well, the tailoring is poor. The clothes you buy should hang well on you, being neither loose nor tight. Invest in a full-length mirror and model your clothes at home before you wear them.

Look in the fashion magazines and in the more expensive stores. Study the clothes that are being sold there. What is the size of the lapel on the men's jackets, how are they buttoning, what is the style of the waistbands and cuff length this year? What is the style of the women's dresses and suits? What are the lengths? What are the popular colors and fabrics? What examples of fashion can be translated into garments that are appropriate for the office? Remember your goal is to have clothing that is fashionable, but projects a conservative businesslike image.

If your budget is somewhat limited, find yourself one of those super discount places that discount name-brand merchandise. Some of these places do not let you return anything so bring a friend with you. I have my favorite places to buy clothes and shoes. I find that by careful shopping I can save about 50 percent on my wardrobe and still have the latest appropriate fashion. Quite often I can tell the brand name. Anyone who wants to check labels in my clothes is going to be disappointed since many of them were cut out before I bought them. I go to the regular store first and determine price and style. Then I go to my favorite places and often find the same merchandise at thirty to fifty percent off. My husband has his favorite places, also, and shops the same way. Because we travel a lot, we have a number of outlets in different parts of the country that are on our good places to shop list. We share names with our friends and tip each other off when we learn of a good sale. It is possible to have a very good-looking wardrobe for less than you are spending now, if you shop carefully and efficiently. You should have certain colors predominate in your wardrobe. When you buy a suit, think of the coordinating blouse or shirt and tie that will go with it. Coordination is especially important in creating an attractive image. If you have problems with colors, and some people are slightly color blind, have a friend help you coordinate your wardrobe.

A conservative, businesslike image may not be the one that you wish to project. At least you may not think so now and indeed it may not be the right one for you. If you want to be a rock star, a kindergarten teacher, a construction engineer or an astronaut you may have to select a wardrobe that reflects a different image. People who work in merchandising have a different set of rules than people who work in laboratories, but both must be aware of how they should dress. There are many new careers you might select that would fit into a less conservative category. The key, however, is that the wardrobe should be appropriate for the position you are seeking to get or seeking to keep.

Some things you may feel are obvious apparently have been forgotten by some individuals I have seen over the years. Clothes should be neat, well-pressed, clean and not show signs of wear, like rings around collars, frayed cuffs, wrinkled jackets and uneven hems. Think of the people who seem to you to be attractive. What is their image? Would you like to project a similar image?

Coordination is an important element. You must look as though you were put together by design and did not just happen. Although some people think women should dress so as to fade into the wood-work, I do not agree with this. Dress for both men and women should never be loud or conspicuous but should be attractive in an understated way. Men who are on the way up dress well and attractively. Shirt, tie and suit are coordinated by color and style. Women should follow the same rules. Colors should be coordinated and styles flattering but not sexy or with a hint of being evening wear. Necklines should not be low. Skirts should not be tight or short.

If you have an important meeting coming up, choose your wardrobe carefully. A camera that develops pictures instantly can be used to help you analyze your image. Have someone take a picture of you in the outfit you have chosen. The camera often reveals much more than the mirror. What image does the outfit project? Is it the one you are seeking to create?

Hair

Long or short, curly or straight, natural or dyed, hair, above all should always be clean. The dandruff commercials get to me at times but they do have a valid message. No matter how attractively you are dressed, the effect will be ruined by dandruff on your collar.

Hair should be an appropriate length and style. What length is appropriate, you may ask? That certainly has varied over the past few years. A woman who wears her hair long will give the image of a little girl. If she is seeking an executive position she is presenting a confusing image. A man who wears his hair long and ties it up in a ponytail is also presenting a different image when he goes seeking a position. A crew cut projects still a different image, which may be as much of a problem as the ponytail in certain situations. Again we have the situation of being "in style" without being too far ahead of the general trend. The fashion magazines are sometimes not much help when it comes to hair. In the women's magazines, at least, hairdos are often wild and not suitable for daily wear. Find a style that is attractive and stay up to date.

Shoes

Shoes, whatever the style, should be polished and have good heels and soles on them. Some feel that women should wear very plain shoes, but I feel an unattractive shoe will take away from an otherwise attractive image. The shoe should not make any sound when you walk. It should not squeak or flip-flop. It should not be an "evening shoe." Men should not generally wear a work shoe or a heavy boot in an office position. There are always exceptions. The important thing is that you are conscious of the image you are trying to project when you choose your footwear.

Glasses

Glasses are a necessity of life for many and that number used to include me. I used to say that I can't find mine without them. This is still true but I have just gotten soft contacts and I love them. It is going to take some conditioning though for me to get out of all those habits I developed while wearing glasses. I have trouble remembering that I have the contact lenses in, I can see so well with them. Contacts, whether hard or soft, are not for everyone.

It always surprises me how many well-groomed, stylish people neglect their eyeglasses. You see people in very attractive outfits with glasses that are discolored, out of style and unflattering. Perhaps the trim is missing. They may have marks on their faces from ill-fitting glasses. They keep pushing them back up on their noses because they do not fit properly. I have even seen them taped together. Your face is the heart of your appearance and your glasses dominate your face. Be certain that they are in good condition. If you have difficulty seeing without your glasses take a friend with you to select frames. It is hard to choose effectively when you can't see.

Accessories

It always somewhat amazes me that a man can fit into his pockets what a woman needs a piece of luggage to carry. A large purse is out of place for a woman in an executive position. Many carry a briefcase that has a section in it to hold the essentials of life. Instead of carrying many things around with you, keep a second set of such necessities as cosmetics and hair spray in the office. A man does not enter a meeting looking as though he is on his way to catch a plane. A woman should not be dragging a heavy purse in addition to her briefcase. Jewelry should be tastefully chosen and not make excessive noise like dangling charm bracelets. Too much jewelry is not appropriate in a many business offices, although this is certainly not true in all cases.

The appropriate briefcase is a consideration for both men and women. It must be large enough to handle what is generally carried to meetings and yet not look like a portable steamer trunk. It should definitely be made of leather and quiet in tone.

Men must consider their own accessories. A belt should be carefully chosen. Wallet and keys should not make an unsightly bulge in your pocket. Jewelry for men is more acceptable than it used to be but it should be chosen with taste.

Posture

The manner in which your clothing hangs is determined, in part, by your posture. Posture is important and may be something you neglect. Try and view yourself in a triple mirror. Do your shoulders hunch over? Does your derriére stick out? There are exercises you can follow to improve your posture. Not only will you look better, you will feel better. You may need to have a friend to give you gentle reminders to straighten up every once in a while.

Personal Habits

There are a number of personal habits that may interfere with your overall image. Biting your nails or touching your face, hair or nose can be negative things that are noticed by others. Chewing gum does not look professional. Smoking is not as accepted as it once was. Think of the little habits you may have developed. Make a short list of them. Do they contribute in a positive way to the image you are trying to create?

THE IMPRESSION YOU MAKE ON OTHERS

The impression you make on others is made up of many factors. You will certainly want to make different impressions on different people and in different circumstances. I act differently with my children than I do with my professional collegues. I dress differently on the weekend than I do on weekdays when I am going to work. When my neighbor sees me getting in the car to go to the tennis courts or to the beach, he certainly gets a different impression of me than when I am either going out for the evening or going to present a technical paper at a meeting. All of these images are valid. I would certainly wear different clothing for each of these affairs. My hair, my shoes, and my general bearing will be different, although my reaction to meeting him might be the same in all three cases. The impression you make on someone is related to your appearance but it is also part of the image you are trying to create.

Whether you are conscious of it or not, you are making an impression on those who meet you. If you are going to create a successful new image, you must be aware of the impression you are creating. It may or may not be the impression you wish to create.

Get out the pencil and paper again and write down four or five different situations that you find yourself in quite often. These should be important to you but vary the situation. They might be such things as "meeting people at a party," "making a formal presentation to my superiors," "interviewing for a new position," "working with my peers," "working with my subordinates," "meeting new customers," "teaching something to children," "meeting new people."

Make each of these situations the heading of a column. Under each heading write down three or four of your characteristics that you would like people to be aware of in the situation identified as the heading of the column. For example, I would like my superiors to be aware of my efficiency and my intelligence but I might like new people I have just met at a party to be aware of my friendliness or attractiveness. My intelligence might or might not be the thing I would like them to be aware of at a first meeting.

There are many ways in which we create certain impressions. Our choice of clothing and our choice of words are certainly very important.

You have identified certain situations in your life and certain impressions you would like to make in each. The next time you are in these situations be conscious of the impression you are making. Is it the one you want to make? What could you do to change things so that you do make the impression you desire to make? Be certain that you are being true to yourself. Is the impression you want to create one that is really you? Creating a false impression can only lead to problems for you. You must be able to carry through on the image you create. You must be comfortable with it.

An interesting experiment was carried out some years ago that demonstrates the effect your image has on the way people respond to you. A tape was made by a doctor on a piece of medical research. The tape was played for three different audiences, the members of each having been selected at random. The tape was introduced differently each time and questions were asked at the conclusion of the tape. The first time, the audience was told that the speaker was an eminent medical researcher, the second time that the speaker was a science writer and the third time that the speaker was a man who had been sent to prison for practicing medicine without a license. The audience who had the first introduction had quite detailed memories of what was said, the audience who had the second introduction remembered some of what had been said, while the third group remembered hardly anything about the lecture. The impression that was planted in their minds by the introduction had a great impact on their reaction to the person on the tape. The impression that you make will also cause people to react to you in different ways.

Speech

Professor Higgins of *My Fair Lady* demonstrated that a person's speech was the key to position in society. This may have been more true in class-conscious England at the turn of the century than in the United States now, but I don't really think so. You will find that people are very aware of the speech of others.

There are two things that must be considered here. One is what you say and the other is how you say it. Some people have a regional or a foreign accent. You may or may not want to change this. There is nothing wrong with having an accent but some accents are considered to be "lower class" or as a sign of illiteracy. I will not try to define what that means, I just know that is the case. We are not talking about what is right, but about the image you are creating. If you want to be considered intelligent, you will have to sound intelligent. This is related to many things including tone of voice, accent, vocabulary and grammar.

For some, there is the matter of tone or placement of voice. Listen to yourself on a tape recorder. Is your voice pleasing? Do you sound nasty, belligerent or friendly and intelligent? Would you like to listen to yourself? There are exercises you can do to develop a more pleasing voice. One factor is learning to place your voice. Many female voices are too high. If you have to make a presentation, tape some of it and listen to the sound of your voice and the way you pronounce your words with special attention to your vowels.

Perhaps an even more important thing to consider is *what* you say. Above all, you must always be grammatically correct. Your vocabulary should be appropriate. Enrich it. Always be certain that you are using words correctly. One way to improve your vocabulary is to read a great deal. Vary what you read. This will not only improve your vocabulary but also give you new things to think about and talk about. Don't let your conversation be nothing but a string of anecdotes.

What do you talk about? Do you monopolize the conversation? One way to make friends and influence people is to be a good listener. Is your conversation dominated by clichés and the recounting of old stories? Is this appropriate? For some situations, it is, for others it is not.

Try to develop a good internal barometer. Think about people whom you see in the kind of position you want to have. What do they talk about? You can't talk about work all the time. You have to be able to carry on light conversation with your associates. This may mean learning about politics, sports or classical music. Whatever you need to do in order to reach proficiency, learn to converse with your associates and those on the level you wish to reach.

If you have to make a presentation, tape it first and listen to a playback of it. What things can you correct? Practice it until you are comfortable with the presentation. You may want to have a friend listen to you on tape, help you analyze your voice and plan any changes you may need to make.

YOU, THE PERSON

Sometimes, in my family when one of us is staring into space we ask "are you in there?" Sometimes the person will answer yes and smile and sometimes there will be no answer because they are too far away in thought.

Who are you inside your body? What is it that no mirror can ever show? Do you know this part of yourself? How do others perceive you? *Personality, psychology,* and *being* are all words that might be used. When you say, "He or she doesn't understand me," what do you mean by the "me"? This is a complicated concept, but one you must understand because it is a very large part of the image.

Do you like yourself? Would you like yourself for a friend, for a fellow worker, for a boss? What parts of you do you like best? What parts of you do you like least?

What would you like to change about your life? What would you like to change about yourself?

Take another piece of paper out and make that list. If you had to change three things about yourself that are not part of appearance but part of your personality, what would you change?

Are you too quiet and shy or are you too loud? Are you generally happy or unhappy? Are you a workaholic or are you lazy? Are you quick or are you slow? Do you make friends easily or only with difficulty? Take that paper and write down five positive things about yourself. Take that same paper and in another column write down five negative things about yourself. How can you build on the positive and eliminate the negative aspects of your personality? If you can change the things that you feel are negative, others will respond to you differently. Many of these characteristics may be important in your search for a new position.

Are you aggressive enough? Are you too aggressive? Will aggressiveness be a plus or a minus in your position? Remember you should be planning for the new career you want, rather than your present situation.

Will "the real you" be happy in the new position? Think about the characteristics that you are happy about. Will these fit in with the characteristics that are needed in your newly chosen career? Changing isn't what's really important. You must change to the right thing.

What values are important to you? You will generally not want to change your value system. Will your old values fit with your new position? Does the image you create fit in with your new value system?

If you are going to create a new image, that image must be able to stand the test of time. It cannot only be a matter of appearance and a few well chosen grammatical phrases. It must go to the heart of your personality. Do others see you as you see yourself? Will others perceive your new image of you? Will it be so different that your old friends and family will not understand it?

You will have to remember that others may not be part of the creation of your new image, nor may they really want you to change. You must be ready for possible rejection of the new image on the part of those who thought they loved the old you. You must be responsive to this situation. You may have some difficult things to overcome. If you are not happy with "the old you" it may be necessary for you to change. You must explain this to those who are close to you. It will not always be easy and you must be prepared to explain your "new self."

In order to do this you must understand it yourself. If you were a naturally shy person and suddenly become very open and talkative, it would be noticed. The reverse is also true. What characteristics of the new image are very important to you and to what you are trying to accomplish? How can you make this clear to those who are close to you? None of us exists in isolation. It is important to remember that.

What image do you present as a worker? What skills are apparent to the person who might be considering hiring you? What impression do you make on an interviewer? Which sides of your personality are most apparent in an interview? Is this the "real" you? Are you projecting something that is not true?

Analyze your image and decide what elements must be changed to create the image you want to project.

You can develop a step-by-step program for creating a new image. It will have componants that relate to your physical characteristics, your appearance, your speech, your work habits and your ideas.

10

Going back to school

Wanting a new position or career is not enough. In order to make a successful career change, you will have to demonstrate that you have the skills required for the new position. In many cases this can be accomplished only through formal education which is a stumbling block for many people. Faced with the necessity of returning to school, some individuals abandon their new goal, rather than obtain the needed training.

Returning to school is not easy. In many cases, however, it is an absolute necessity. When you are changing careers, you are at a disadvantage.

1. You may not have the skills necessary to carry out the position.
2. You may not know you do not have the skills or even what the needed skills are.
3. You may not have a method for documenting that you do indeed have the needed skills for the position.

The employer who hires a young person straight out of school has a record and academic references to use as part of the hiring assessment.

This individual has current knowledge in the field in which he/she is being hired. Both the employer and the employee make some assumptions that the proper preparation for the position has taken place, placing some security in the academic program that prepared and certified the student.

The person who is involved in a career change brings a different set of credentials, which in many cases look a little bit like Swiss cheese. There is some substance is of high quality, but there are also a lot of holes.

The role of an academic institution, whether it be a college or some form of vocational school, is more complex than the potential student sometime realizes.

"The school teaches me what I need to know," you say. "It gives me a degree." This phrase is absolutely true, but it implies much more than you may realize.

If you are planning to make a career change, there are a number of questions you will have to answer.

1. Do I need additional formal training?
2. What kind of training do I need?
3. What is the best place I can go to get that training?
4. What do I have to do to prepare myself and my family for the emotional reality of my going back to school?
5. What skills will I need if I am returning to school?

Although some discussion of these questions is presented in this chapter, the reader who wants a more extensive preparation on these topics should refer to my book, *Are You Ready?: A Survival Manual for Women Returning to School*. Although the title implies that the book is for women, much of the material included is quite valid for men as well.

DO YOU NEED ADDITIONAL FORMAL TRAINING?

There are certain authors who have written about career change who either imply or state directly that you do not need to take formal training for a career change. These statements may be encouraging to some who want to plunge into their newly selected area, but I cannot help believe that this is false encouragement. In most cases, although indeed not in all, preparation in the new area is certainly needed. Let us think about some possible examples, which may be related to some of the items in magazine articles you may have read on the subject.

You have been doing volunteer work, organizing individuals and collecting a substantial amount of money for charity. You are now able to put this on your résumé as a qualification and are prepared to enter the world of business as a manager. It is true that this accomplishment will help fill out your résumé, but it will never replace "real" work experience and/or an MBA. You may say this experience gave you far more opportunity and responsibility than you would ever have had in a work position. That may be the case. Right and reason, however, have not yet replaced reality. The person who has been in the work force in a job directly related to the one being sought will have a distinct advantage over the person who has not held such a position. The person who has just finished an educational program directly related to the position being sought also has an advantage, his or her skills are up to date.

You often hear the complaint, particularly among young people, "I can't get a job without experience and I can't get the experience." That may be an unfortunate truth but you can arrange to reinforce your academic preparation, at the very least.

It is true you may not need to attend college or get an advanced degree to get certain positions, but you are severely limiting yourself in potential development of a career.

Many individuals have chosen to attend a technical school or vocational school and found that they were well prepared for the starting position in their chosen field. They often also find that they can't get promoted to higher level positions, however. Experience is a good teacher, but she is no substitute for credentials. With credentials you can get experience. Without credentials, you may only get lower-level experience.

There are some areas in which you can demonstrate your ability without going to school. If you are seeking a career in an area which demands creative skills, you will have to prepare a portfolio. This will include samples of your work—photography, writing, layouts, designs, art work or whatever. It is possible to maintain and even develop further skills in creative areas without attending formal classes. In some cases, formal academic training inhibits creativity, while in others it can advance knowledge and technique. If you are going to use the portfolio route rather than documentation of recent formal education be certain that your portfolio looks professional. It should follow the form which graduates of the formal program are instructed to follow. You could check with a recent graduate of a formal program or from an instructor in the program. Some of them may be interested in helping you a little even though you are not able to enter their program, if they feel you have talent and you broach the question in the correct manner.

Many people feel that because they can do something they are able to teach it. This is sometimes not true. Teaching is a skill in itself. Knowledge of a field is not all you need. You will need some training in the method of teaching your subject as well as in interpersonal relations with your students. In particular, you may have to meet specific reuirements in order to teach. They differ according to geographic location, grade level and the subject matter involved. Your local school board and/or department of education at a local college can tell you how to find out about the requirements which would apply to you. Even if courses in teaching are not required, you may be well advised to take them.

Are you up to date in the field of your choice? This is the key question. What does a recent graduate know about the field you have chosen? You can find this out by taking a look at the courses that are offered and at the books used for those courses. Do you know most of the material? Are you comfortable with it? Can you use all the jargon of the field? If the answer is an unqualified yes then you may not need any additional education, but do not fool yourself on this crucial question. You may be able to fool your future employer long enough to get the job, but how will you perform?

Are your skills up to an appropriate performance standard? This may include operating some piece of equipment. There have been many changes in some equipment: the computer is taking over the world, word processing is revolutionizing many areas and even typewriters have undergone significant changes.

Are you limiting your opportunities by depending on outdated skills and knowledge?

Could you open up brand new areas for yourself if you did go back to school? Are you eliminating something from your list of possibilities because of the fact that you would have to go back to school to accomplish it?

If you are satisfied with your knowledge and skill level you may not need to go back to school. Make that decision with full knowledge of yourself and your opportunities, however.

If you do decide to take a course or a program, you should begin your decision-making process with the question of the right curriculum and then select the school that will give you that curriculum.

THE CURRICULUM

Although accrediting bodies and professional organizations have some input, you must remember that the schools design curricula. Different courses are chosen, majors developed and a degree given by a particular institution. The institution may use guidelines provided by accrediting agencies or state departments of education or professional associations, but it still has great freedom. Curricula at two different institutions may be quite similar but this is not always the case. Curriculum at one institution may be very current and at another it may not have changed essentially in twenty years. This is true of colleges and universities, as well as professional and vocational schools. Not all degrees lead to a career. This is an important thing to remember. This is not the fault of the institution, nor a flaw in the program. Many students have followed a particular major only to discover that they could not get a job using their knowledge when they graduated. Remember that there are reasons for choosing a particular major other than preparing for a career but this important to many.

The university has a responsibility to provide education and maintain knowledge about areas of scholarship which are somewhat unique and not necessarily job related. There are many courses of study that are important in themselves but may not be job related. It is for you to determine if a particular course of study will lead to the career you want. Just getting a college degree, for example, will not open up all doors for you, although it will open some.

Curricula at different schools are different. Some people believe that if you are taking the same major at two different schools you will have basically the same program. This is not generally true. Study and compare curricula for the same program title. Are the requirements the same?

If you find that you went to the wrong school or if you find you took the wrong program, you may try to blame in part the counseling service of the institution. You must really look to yourself. You have to be responsible for planning your college program. You will have to be aggressive in asking questions and making comparisons. This move is yours.

CERTIFICATION
AND ACCREDITATION

One role that a learning institution plays is as a certifying body. The university certifies that you have certain knowledge in specific areas. The credibility of the university reflects on you. If the institution you attended has a very good reputation, you will generally be a more desirable job candidate. Never let anyone tell you that it doesn't matter from where you graduate as long as you have a college degree. That is far from true.

An important element is the accreditation of the institution itself. All institutions are not of the same quality. In order to monitor the performance of schools and universities, accrediting agencies have been formed. Dividing the country into regions, these accrediting agencies work together and exchange information. Schools in one region will accept the accreditation of an institution made by the agency in their own region or by one of the other accrediting agencies. If you are going to attend a college, be certain that it has been *ACCREDITED* by one of the regional accrediting agencies. Some schools that are not accredited try to tell you that accreditation doesn't matter. It does. Credits obtained at a college that is not accredited may not be accepted by an accredited school if you transfer. Quality varies even among accredited schools. Be cautious, you are dealing with your future.

If you want to check on an institution, call or write to the accrediting agency for your region. You can probably get the current address and the name of the executive director from your library. The six major accrediting agencies and the states they represent are:

Middle States Asssociation of Colleges and Secondary Schools: Delaware, District of Columbia, Maryland, New Jersey, New York, Pennsylvania, Canal Zone, Puerto Rico, Virgin Islands.

New England Association of Schools and Colleges: Connecticut, Maine, Masachusetts, New Hampshire, Rhode Island, Vermont.

North Central Association of Colleges and Secondary schools: Arizona, Arkansas, Colorado, Illinois, Indiana, Iowa, Kansas, Michigan, Minnesota, Missouri, Nebraska, New Mexico, North Dakota, Ohio, Oklahoma, South Dakota, West Virginia, Wisconsin, Wyoming.

Northwest Association of Secondary and Higher Schools: Alaska, Idaho, Montana, Nevada, Oregon, Utah, Washington.

Southern Association of Colleges and Schools: Alabama, Florida, Georgia, Kentucky, Louisiana, Mississippi, North Carolina, South Carolina, Tennessee, Texas, Virginia.

Western Association of Colleges and Schools: California and Hawaii.

In addition to verifying the accreditation of the institution, you should determine if the specific career for which you are preparing requires a license or a special accreditation on the part of the program. Will the program you are entering qualify you to sit for licensing exams? In some cases programs may be applying for this specialized accreditation. Identify the program status and its significance. For example, courses to be used to obtain a teaching license must be approved by the Department of Education of the state in which you are seeking to be licensed. Many professional programs must be accredited by their respective professional associations.

Don't assume things. Find out if your school and program are properly accredited before you enter.

SELECTING THE CORRECT PROGRAM

If you have already selected a new career, your problems in selecting a specific program will be somewhat reduced. If there is more than one accredited institution in your area, compare the programs carefully. You may not want to enter a college program. Think this out carefully. A vocational program may appear to be the appropriate one for you. Consider it well, however. How do employers react to someone applying for the desired position who does not have a college degree and/or experience in the field? Remember, you will be viewed differently than a young person starting out. If you already have a degree you have credentials. This is important. If you do not have a degree, you may want to consider the extra time needed to get one as a good investment. Many students who have completed a technical program and decided later that they wanted a degree have found that their work in a non-accredited technical or vocational school was not accepted for transfer to a college. Determine all of these factors before you make your final program selection.

Remember that not all courses offered by a university are for credit. Not all courses offered by one program in a university are accepted for transfer credit in another program of the same university. This is a reasonable academic rule but has been a terrible surprise to many students.

Another important thing to investigate is the level of position you can obtain in the field of your choice with the degree you are seeking. For example, there are not very many positions for bachelor's degree graduates in psychology or in physics. Most positions in these areas require advanced training. There are, however, high level positions for those with bachelor's degrees in engineering, computer science and business. This situation may change, of course, but the change would be in the direction of a greater emphasis on education. Be sure to determine exactly what you need to get the position you are seeking.

ADMISSIONS

After you have selected the school and the program, you will have to consider what you must do to gain admittance to the program. Admission requirements vary according to the institution and sometimes within programs in the same institutions.

Some universities require that you submit scores from the College Board Entrance Exams or Standard Aptitude Tests. These are given several times a year at specific locations. You cannot just show up at one of the exam centers. You must make a reservation by a specific date. The guidance office at a nearby high school can give you information concerning this exam, or you can write directly to The College Board, 888 Seventh Avenue, New York, New York, 10019. If you desire to enter a college or university which requires this exam you will have to make your preparations many months in advance. You will see a requirement for S.A.T. scores on some application forms. These are the same thing.

When you register for this exam, you will get a little booklet containing some sample questions and answers. These seem simple but don't let them fool you. You may not have taken this type of exam for a while. *Study for it*...I can not say this too strongly. The people who make up the exam say you can't study for it, but that is not true. Purchase one or more of the books that are written to help on these exams. They are available at most bookstores and can be special ordered for you by the others. These books contain sample questions and sample tests. The test includes a verbal part and a mathematical part. In addition, there are specialized subject matter tests. Take the tests and time yourself. You may be able to answer the questions but it may take you too much time. The score you get on this exam may determine whether or not you will get into the program of your choice. Optimize your opportunity to do well.

Some institutions have open admissions policies. This means that you will not have to take an entrance exam. It does not mean that you can do poorly in your work once you have entered the institution.

If you have an admission interview, be open about your reasons for returning to school. Your motivation may be an important factor in the decision about whether to admit you. Although some schools do not have waiting lists, others do. Do not give up if you are rejected at one instititon. Waiting lists are very valid instruments. Just because you see articles about the buyers market for students, do not think this is the case at all colleges. If you are rejected by a number of different institutions, ask those schools why you were turned down. This is very important information.

LEARNING STYLES

If you do get in, can you do the work? This is the question that many students ask themselves. The answer sometimes prompts students to drop out before they even start. There are many elements involved when one is returning to school. There is the family situation, the question of time management, the survival under stress and there is the sharpening of basic skills.

In *Are You Ready?* I devote a number of pages to the elements that are involved in your making the decision to return to school, and to steps that will help you and your family make the adjustment. I will not cover those elements here, but it is appropriate to speak about stress.

Stress is a prominent component of present-day living. In an earlier chapter, a table was presented that indicated a value for various stress elements in our lives. Changing careers is definitely stressful. If you have to add the element of returning to school to this, you will increase stress.

In order to minimize this component, you must take every opportunity to make things easier for yourself. This includes such things as visiting the campus in advance of your first class in order to identify the location of all the places you need to find on your first days. It very definitely includes improving your skills in a number of areas. You will have to learn how to read for information, how to write a term paper, how to take tests and how to use the library.

Going to college involves interaction with fellow students. If you are substantially older than the other students in your classes you will have to develop a technique for interacting with them. Do not assume that because you are older, you will not fit into your classes. The average age at academic institutions has been creeping upward over the last few years. The local state institution in my community quotes twenty-eight years as their average age. Since I know they serve a number of eighteen to twenty-two year olds this means that they must have a large number of students at the other end of the scale as well. Times are changing rapidly and you may be surprised to see the makeup of the classes you are attending.

A basic element in your success in college will be your preparation in the basic skills. Particularly, mathematics will be important for a number of programs and these skills must be at your fingertips and confidence is imperative here. Perhaps even more important than mathematics is your ability to communicate. Your ability to read, write and speak effectively will determine not only your success in your academic program but your fate in your new field. There are few areas in which communication is not a vital ingredient but these areas generally depend on the degree of development of another skill. You may want to be a fine dancer, mechanic, artist and whatever. You may or may not need to develop what is generally termed communication for your particular field but you will need it if you are to be successful as a person.

Returning to school will make many demands on you. You must realize this. You will have to be prepared to modify your life, to devote the needed time to your family, your work and your school work. This is not a trivial problem.

Returning to school is not a casual thing. It must be planned. For some, this planning must be done well in advance of the starting date of classes, it should begin by developing the basic skills.

It is not unusual to be afraid when thinking about returning to school. The fear of failure can keep you from even starting. Think about all the things you must do to prepare for college and do the preparation.

Pick the right program in the right college.

Learn your way around the school and make friends with your fellow students.

Improve your communication skills.

Learn to write papers since many of your grades will depend on your ability to produce research papers.

Plan a time schedule that will allow you to get your academic work finished on time and yet leave a piece of your life for your family and for living in general.

11

Communication skills

Remember the three "R's"? Reading, writing, and rithmetic are three skills that you will obviously need if you are going to undertake any kind of educational program. You realize this, I am certain. You may tell me your math is a little rusty but of course you can read and write. You learned to read and write in grammar school just like everyone else. Please take a good look at your ability to read and write. College will make very strenuous demands on these abilities.

The fact is that not everyone learns to read and write, and some people cannot read on a level which is needed for them to perform successfully in college or other specialized schools.

But you have been reading and writing, you will say. You read the newspaper, novels and occasionally even the cereal box. You write lists, and letters to your mother and Aunt Tilly. As meritorious as all those things may be, they do not completely prepare you for entering those hallowed halls.

Many positions in industry require that you comprehend complex material, but employers complain that they are faced with potential employees who cannot even fill out employment applications. Individuals who are changing careers often find they must obtain some additional education or training before they can obtain their new position. This may be in a college, a vocational school or in a training program in a company. In all cases it demands a high level of reading proficiency.

Reading in college is marked by the volume of material you have to digest, the level on which it is written and the amount of information you have to obtain from the printed page.

I am not trying to frighten you, but even those who are omnivorous readers of light material find they have problems when they try to keep up with their college assignments. A friend of mine, who, like me, reads every piece of print in sight including the cereal box on the breakfast table, found herself pressed when she went back to get her Master's degree in library science. She discovered she had to give up her light reading during that period. Light reading and heavy reading are such different techniques that she found that she could not get involved with both at the same time. Even if you are a good reader, you may find that the same is true.

Before you can improve your reading ability you have to assess just where you are. There are many components to reading that must be evaluated separately. A number of tests are designed to do this and many are related to a certain grade level in school. There are programs all over the country, some private and some public which can help you assesss and remediate your reading ability.

Colleges have introduced remedial reading programs to help incoming students. Open admission policies in some schools allow students to enter on the basis of having graduated from high school, but shocking results have been produced on some of the reading assessment tests. A frightening percentage of incoming freshmen reading on the third to sixth grade level. Do you think that you might fall into that group? Even if you are not in that position you might find that you do not test as well as you think you will.

Before you enter testing and remediation programs, let us do some self-assessment. The reading components that we will discuss are comprehension, vocabulary, speed, and timing.

READING COMPREHENSION

Comprehension is the most important of these components for the college student.The word itself means understanding, and reading without understanding is a useless task. It doesn't matter how fast you read if you don't understand what you are reading. It is a little bit like the story about the driver who had taken the wrong road. He said he was lost but he was making great time.

To have good comprehension you must understand not only the meaning of the individual words, but also the meaning of the words when they are used together. There may be implications, as well as information, that must be gained from a phrase or paragraph. You will have to not only improve your understanding of words but your understanding of words grouped together. This is a case where the whole is greater than the sum of the parts.

How can you evaluate your ability to comprehend material? First of all, you must identify the kinds of material you will be using in the program you will enter. You can do this by getting the titles of the books you would be using from the bookstore. If you do not want to buy books in advance, you can then check out the same or similar books from the library. Read a section of the book and try to do some of the following things. Find a title for the section you have just read. This should indicate the point of the material. Write a topic sentence which summarizes the material. Take each paragraph on a page and try to summarize it in a single sentence. If you are having difficulty doing this, try rephrasing the sentences in a single paragraph on a sentence-by-sentence basis. If you can rephrase material you probably understand it. If you cannot, you probably are unsure of it.

Make a list of the factual items included in the material. If you are able to get a book that has questions at the end of the chapter, try to read a section and *without looking up the material*, answer the questions.

How do you know if you have done well? For the factual information you can check the answers with the material in the text. The evaluation of the summary, title and topic sentence will require the assistance of someone who has been successful in similar courses. You can, with practice, gain confidence as you learn, but you may need some initial help.

Retention is another component which is closely related to comprehension. Comprehension measures what you understand. Retention measures how long you remember what you have read or studied.

You may be interested in getting an idea of your grade level for comprehension, or some of the other components of reading, without taking a formal test. The following process will give you a very rough—and I do mean rough—approximation. Grade level refers to an average specific ability level for children. Some children read far above their grade level. Other children read below grade level and they continually fall farther behind as they move from grade to grade. Textbooks are written using a specific grade level of reading which may be at or below the grade level for which the book is written. For example, there may be two social studies books written for use in the sixth grade. One of these may be written for a sixth-grade level reader and one may be written for a fourth-grade level reader.

To get an approximate idea of your reading level, obtain some textbooks which give some indication of the grade level. If you have children in school, you may be able to use some of their books or one of their teachers may help you obtain some for the grade level you desire. The school librarian or the principal may also help you if you explain your plan. In larger school systems there is generally a library for teachers to obtain materials. You might try there. Some libraries also have books which are graded according the reading level. The children's librarian may be of help to you.

Find the level of the books with which you are really comfortable. These may be high school texts written on a twelfth grade level or they may be far below that level. This will give you a rough approximation. Sometimes this is not indicated in the book itself but the teacher who loans you the book would be able to tell you the grade level for which it was written. It will be indicated in the teacher's manual he or she has with the book. A far better technique would be to be tested using one of the standard reading tests. There are a number which have been designed for use by adults.

VOCABULARY

All of us have a number of different vocabularies. For example, there is our speaking vocabulary, our reading vocabulary and our writing vocabulary. We use different words depending on our subject matter and the context. We use a different vocabulary when speaking to a small child than we would use in writing a formal report.

If you work to increase your reading recognition vocabulary you will also be increasing your written vocabulary. Make an investment in a pocket dictionary, carry it with you and *read* it. You can learn a new word while you are waiting for the light to change or for a line to move. You would have a magnificent vocabulary if you had done that during some of the gas crisis lines. Keep a list of your new words and keep going over them. As a word becomes part of both your reading and writing vocabulary, you can remove it from your working list.

Every subject matter has its own vocabulary, its own jargon. Be certain you know the jargon of the subject you are going to study. Again, you can get a college level textbook in the subject matter. This time, go to the index in the back of the book. Be certain that you know the meaning of every word in the index. To "know" the meaning means you can write a definition in your own words, not that you sort of remember hearing the word used at some time, and that you can use it. Look up new words and add them to your vocabulary list. As they become part of your vocabulary, you can remove them from the list.

SPEED

You may have seen ads for increasing your reading speed. Remember that comprehension is more important but you cannot neglect speed. You will have a substantial amount of material to read and only a limited amount of time. If you can increase your reading speed, with full comprehension, you will have effectively increased the number of hours in your day.

Your rate of reading will be related to the difficulty of the material. You will read a textbook much more slowly than a *Reader's Digest* article. Try a test to find out how fast you can read "ordinary" material. To do this you need a watch with an alarm or a friend who will watch the clock for you. Take a magazine article with average vocabulary. Count the number of words on five lines and divide your answer by five. You will then have an average value for the number of words per line. Have someone time you for sixty seconds while you read at your regular reading speed. You will then have to count the number of lines you have read during this minute. Multiply the number of lines by the average number of words per line and you will have the number of words read in a minute. How do you know the meaning of your rate (your wpm is the number of words you read per minute)?

There are some general parameters which vary according to reading program but the ones I use for light reading are:

200 wpm or below	poor
300 wpm	average
400 wpm	good
over 500	excellent

Now that you have your speed calculated for light reading, try the same thing with textbook material. The numbers above are not infalliable. If you come out high on the scale, you can assume you are reading light material at a good rate. You can always increase that, however. If you come out with a poor score, you should definitely include a reading improvement program in your future. If you cannot take an official program, there are several things you can do to improve your rate of reading speed.

Practicing your reading will serve to improve your speed. One of the first things you have to do is to find out what is slowing you down. Knowing how to read each word is only a part of reading. You also have to learn to put the words together. This puts us into the question of timing.

If you read one word at a time, you will not only be slow, you will also be reducing your comprehension. In order to make gains in both areas, you will have to learn to first read a couple of words at a time and then whole phrases.

A rather obvious, but sometimes neglected, solution is to have your eyes examined. Eyesight that was adequate for daily living may not be sharp enough for all the reading you will be doing.

Another problem that people have is one of letting the eyes go back over the words that have just been read. The eyes and then the mind are reading and rereading. It is as is as if you were were going over going over the same thing same thing over and over. Think of how much extra time it would take you to read a page if you read like that. You might not do quite as much over-reading as shown above but most people are not aware of just how much they really do.

If you read a story out loud you know that it takes you much longer than if you read it to yourself. Some people unconsciously move their lips when they are reading and this slows them down. The movement may be very subtle. To determine if this is one of your habits, put your finger near your mouth when you are reading and see if you can detect any movement. If you find that you are guilty of this, practice reading with your finger on your lips until you rid yourself of this habit.

If you find that you are an average reader and wish to increase your rate, try pacing yourself. Set a task, in this case a number of words per minute, that is a little bit larger than your normal amount. Try and read a little more than you would read, on the average, in a five-minute period. Do this until you are comfortable and you will be reading at a your new rate. You should maintain the same level of comprehension at this new rate. You will gradually raise your reading speed, but do not fool yourself. You are not reading faster if you are understanding less because you are not really reading, you are just looking at words.

There are many books written to improve your reading. My book *Are You Ready?: A Survival Manual for Women*, has a more extensive section than has been presented here. If you are seriously interested in improving your reading, purchase or get a library copy of one of the many books that have been written specifically to do this. The time you spend on improving your reading ability will be returned to you over and over again. You may even find that you will now enjoy reading even if you had been a "non-reader" before.

WRITING

One of the main activities of college students seems to be writing papers. Desperate, panic in their eyes, they will answer your inquiry into their state of desperation with, "I have to do a paper."

This is something new to many adults. When they went to high school they did not learn to write papers. But times have changed. My children are starting their first research paper in the fifth grade, complete with bibliography. This will make life easier for them when they get to college, but I suppose something else will be thought up for them to do by that time. College professors complain that young people, who should have learned it in high school, still don't know how to write a paper either. In any case it is a task that will become very familiar before you graduate from college. Vocational programs do not usually require as many papers as college programs but improving your skill in writing will still improve your success as a job applicant in many areas.

There are several steps you must follow when doing a paper.

1. choose a topic
2. establish a timetable
3. obtain and use research materials
4. record and make notes on the material
5. find a pivotal point of view
6. write the paper
7. prepare the footnotes and the bibliography
8. type the paper
9. submit the paper on time

You may have a topic specifically assigned by the professor, but usually, you have some flexibility in the selection of a topic. Hopefully, there will be enough material on an assigned topic for you to complete a successful paper. If you are selecting your own topic, this may not necessarily be the case. If you are able to change your own topic, be certain that there is enough material before you commit yourself to it.

It is possible to write a paper that is just one long string of facts and opinions. It won't be a very good paper, however. It will just be a long clothesline of facts and/or opinions strung out for the reader to see. Incidently you should be very clear in distinguishing between fact and opinion. It is not difficult to recognize facts as facts. A name, a date, a documented, observed incident is a fact. Many things that are considered to be facts are really opinions. The fact that something has been written by a prominant person does not make it a fact. It is usually still just an opinion. There is no problem with including your own opinion or the opinion of others in your writing as long as you indicate it as such. You must also give a proper reference to the source of the opinion as well as for any facts which you may include.

It is important for your paper to have structure. It may seem obvious, but your paper must have a beginning, a middle and an end. Each of these parts doesn't just happen. Your paper must have more than a topic. It must have a pivotal point or central point which is the focus of the whole paper. The selection of this pivotal point and its substantiation is the key to a successful paper.

The beginning of the paper must have an opening sentence, which sets the tone for the remainder of the paper and states the main point. It should be well written and perhaps revised a number of times.

The end is not just the last part of the paper. It is the summing up, the conclusion. It is, in one sense, a rewording of the first part.

The middle part of the paper is just that. This is the section in which you put the facts, opinions, etc. that you are going to use to substantiate your premise or main point. Papers have been summarized as having the following steps: You tell what you are going to do, you do it, and you tell what you did. Too many papers just reach an end. They don't have a proper summary. If you look at a paper that wasn't successful, you will find that it probably didn't have a good structure. You may find that it didn't have a single key point. While it is possible to support a major point and some minor points in the same paper, you cannot support several major points successfully. You also cannot have a successful paper without a main point.

Simple, clear writing is always the most effective. Writing teachers will tell you that over and over, but somehow it doesn't always seem to "take". If you are asked to do a creative writing assignment, you are often told to write about something you know. Be certain to follow the rules of grammer, spelling and punctuation. I keep a little pocket book of 20,000 words next to my typewriter so that I can check the spelling of a word without having to get out my big dictionary. This investment of $1.45 has saved me much effort and the embarassment of having misspelled words in my writing. Be very clear about the rules of grammar and punctuation. Are you writing complete sentences? That is a very common error. Are you comfortable with the rules of grammar and the parts of speech? There are many excellent self-instructional books on the rules of grammar, which will help you review or learn these all-important rules for the first time.

There are very formal rules for footnotes and bibliographical entries. Manuals have been written that have slightly different forms. Most colleges have adopted one of these manuals as their official style manual. Some departments use different forms, which are related to the forms used by the professional journals for that discipline. Be certain you know the correct form before you type your paper.

Whatever you do, type your paper. This chapter is entitled communication, and the manner in which you present your work is part of this communication. If it is handwritten, dirty etc. you are displaying lack of interest and respect for the course. Some professors will not take a paper unless it is typed.

There are many aspects of a paper which must be planned. Not the least of these is your schedule to write it. When you are given the assignment date, pretend it is a week earlier and have your paper finished early. You may not be able to get books from the library or find other resource material if you wait until the last minute. It really won't take you any more time to finish it early.

This is by no means a complete description of how to write a paper. It also does not tell you everything you need to know about the art of writing itself. These are each topics for entire books and even series of books. This section is intended to point out to you some of the basic points which you must recognize and to direct you to further sources.

SPEECH AND OTHER FORMS OF COMMUNICATION

You communicate with your speech, by the tone of your voice and by body language. Your grammar, the pitch of your voice, the way you sit are all parts of communication. Listen to yourself on tape. Are you pleasant to listen to? Everyone thinks that the tape distorts them but the distortion is far less than we imagine. "That doesn't sound like me," is the instant reaction of everyone when they hear themselves on tape for the first time. It probably is a lot closer to what you sound like than you imagine.

What do you sound like? What kind of an impression do you make on others? Poor grammar is translated by the listener into "this person is not very smart." Be smart, be "grammar perfect."

Think of the other qualities you project with your body language. Are you secure, insecure, aggressive, proud, beautiful, etc? Many of your characteristics are projected not by what you say, but by how you say it and your attitude or body language as you say it.

To others, you are what you communicate. Part of the change you must make is to improve your ability to communicate with others.

12

Summing up yourself
—the résumé

In order to resume you must have a résumé. That seems like a sentence that one might have thought up for a game of charades or some kind of question in a *New York Times* crossword puzzle. There really is quite a bit more to the relationship between the two words than an accident or incident, if you will, of spelling.

I must admit that I never thought of the link between the two words, *résumé* used as a noun with the accent omitted in most cases of it and *resume*, used as a verb. The use of the French word seems so elegant, so polished, so cosmopolitan. It adds a certain element of class to that piece of paper that reduces your life, your successes, your failures and your dreams to a few lines to be interpreted by the reader.

A résumé is directly related to the importance of the position you are seeking. It is an outline of your experiences, your education and your aptitudes. A person applying just for a job does not generally have a résumé. He or she fills out an application, of course, but "just a job" does not generally require a résumé. A career does require this, whether you are beginning a career, changing careers or continuing your present one. The product you submit as your résumé reflects not only your training, your ability and your experiences, but also your attitude toward these things. It is the vehicle by which you sell yourself.

To resume is to begin again. It implies that one has started before, made some gains, shown some progress, has taken a respite for whatever reason, and is now ready to continue. This element of continuity is difficult for the person who is seeking their first position. "How can you get a job if you haven't had a job?" This question is often heard among young people. The problem is equally true for older people who are seeking to change or begin careers later in life. "How can you begin a career when you haven't had experience?"

At no time does a lack of relevant experience seem more like a stone wall than when you are trying to put together your résumé. "How can your write a résumé when you haven't had any experiences?"

The résumé creates an impression of you that may determine not only whether or not you get the position you seek, but whether you even get an interview for that position. You must decide what you want to project through this résumé. Among a great number of other things, you certainly want to project the virtues of cleanliness, tidiness and somewhat understated attractiveness. You also want to ensure that your résumé is read. You want your résumé to be looked at for positive reasons.

These criteria determine certain things about the appearance of a résumé. Some rules have developed and, whether or not you agree with them, you should follow them. You may have very specific ideas about the appearance of your résumé and you may be right, for your particular case, but in almost every instance, the following relationships hold up.

1. A résumé should measure 8½ x 11 inches.
2. A résumé should be perfectly typed with no (absolutely no!) spelling errors or typographical errors. This rule applies even if the position includes no typing requirement.
3. A résumé should be reproduced on a very high quality copier on good bond paper so that it is almost indistinguishable from the original. You can have your resume printed or bondpaper can be used in high quality reproduction equipment. Word processors do beautiful work on résumés. Never use ditto or spirit masters for a résumé. That is a disaster. If you submit an original of your résumé, don't think it will be returned in a good condition so that it can be used again. It never is.

4. A résumé should be printed on white paper or on a very soft cream color (off-white). There are many people who will tell you to print your résumé on colored paper in order to make it stand out among a pile of other résumés. Although it is important to "stand out," it is also important that you stand out for the right reason. You should stand out because of a certain element of professionalism, of "class", rather than for gaudiness—unless this fits with the career you have chosen.

If you are sending a letter with the résumé, it should also be expertly typed on white or off-white 8½ x 11 inch stationery. Mass-produced résumés are acceptable if done on a good machine, but letters should always be originals. Each company with which you communicate should feel it is the "only one." A multicopied letter is never regarded in the same manner as an original. Would you send a photocopy of a love letter? Again, a word processor is a marvelous solution to the multiple letter problem.

There are a number of different types of letters you may write.

1. Inquiry letter
2. Letter in response to position announcement
3. Résumé letter
4. Thank-you letter
5. Letter in response to offer

The blind inquiry letter is perhaps the most difficult to write. This letter introduces you to a company and allows you to inquire about open positions that may fit with the talents you describe in the résumé which accompanies the letter. In order to properly write this letter you must know quite a bit about the company and the positions which it may have open now or at a future date. Some positions are never advertised. Positions may be created to make use of available talent. You do not want to eliminate yourself from a possible position with either a completely ambiguous letter or an overly specific letter. The letter should be brief, well typed, and should state some of your employment goals. You can find out a great deal about a company from the reference section of your public library. You may also be able to look back through the want ads of your local paper and review the positions they have had open in the past.

The letter in response to a position announcement, whether it be one you obtain from a placement office or from a newspaper or

```
                              333 Angle Worm Cove
                              Misty Harbor, MA  02177
                              April 6, 1981

     Director of Personnel
     Atlas Manufacturing, Inc.
     555 Main St.
     East Lynn, MA  02178

     Dear Sir:

          A teacher for a number of years, I have recently
     directed my interests toward the training of adults.
     Currently I am a candidate for the Masters in Human Resource
     Management degree at the University of Massachussetts
     (Boston campus).

          Your recent expansion of personnel indicates to me
     that you will need to expand your training staff.  I believe
     I am the right person to fill your training needs.  I have
     attached a résumé and will call in a week for an appointment
     for an interview.

                              Yours truly,

                              Harold Edgerton
                              Harold Edgerton
```

Inquiry Letter

professional journal, should also be brief, especially if it is accompanied
by a résumé. You have two alternatives here. You may choose to
summarize the aspects of your résumé you believe will convince the
reader he or she should interview you for the position. Or you may
write a simpler letter expressing your interest and availability for an
interview and attach the résumé. Your statements should be brief and to
the point. Obviously, the grammar should be flawless and the typing
should be perfect.

　　You may state some reasons you are interested in the position or
why you feel your background is appropriate. If your résumé basically
consists of background in non-related fields, you might want to state
your reasons for believing that you can fill the position in the inquiry

```
                                        334 North Ridge Drive
                                        Happy Dale, PA  44444
                                        March 4, 1981

        Managing Editor
        Happy Dale Free Press
        31 Main St.
        Happy Dale, PA  44445

        Dear Sir:

            I am writing in response to your advertisement for a
        writer to take over the "Happy Doings" column in your
        weekly paper and to do additional feature writing.

            My writing skills, my educational background in
        journalism, and my strong interest in people make me the
        right candidate for the position.

            A freelance writer for the past five years, I have had
        a number of articles published, many of which can be
        categorized as human interest.  I have a Bachelors degree
        from State University with a major in English, and my
        studies included a number of courses in journalism.

            I am enclosing a résumé and copies of two of my latest
        articles.  I will bring a larger sampling of my work to an
        interview.

                                        Yours truly,

                                        Pennelope Harris
                                        Pennelope Harris
```

Letter in Response to Position Announcement

letter. You would not want the reviewer to think that you didn't
understand the requirements for the position. In this case, it is
sometimes better to write a strong inquiry letter containing some
résumé elements and basically directed toward the reasons the position
interests you and the strengths you will bring to the job. In this type of
letter you do not enclose a résumé, but state that one is available on

request. You may get a better response than if you attach a weak or inappropriate résumé.

The résumé letter is one that presents your résumé in a somewhat directed manner. Key headings from your résumé, such as education, experience and goals, are addressed in a less formal manner than in your résumé. Neither your complete educational background or work background need be included here. Gaps will not be as noticable as they may be in a formal résumé. Be certain you have not written the résumé letter, however, so that it appears there is only one position for which you may be qualified. You may be unknowingly eliminating yourself from another (better?) position of which you are not aware.

The thank-you letter is more than just something you send to Aunt Tillie to thank her for the birthday present she sent you. It can be very effective and cause an interviewer to remember you. It might be the very thing that causes your résumé to be pulled from a pile.

Thank-you Letter

```
                                      555 North Elm St.
                                      Farmingdale, NY  21200
                                      April 17, 1981

    Mr. Charles Harris
    IBM Corp.
    Peekskill, NY  33333

    Dear Mr. Harris:

         Thank you for the opportunity to interview for the
    position of systems analyst and for the tour of the IBM
    facility.

         The professionalism of the company has always
    interested me and after reviewing the information you
    presented to me, I find that I am quite interested in
    becoming a member of your project team.

                              Yours truly,
```

Persistence, something short of "nagging," is vital to the obtaining of a new position. A very simple letter expressing your appreciation for the interview and continued interest in the position will once more bring your name to the attention of the interviewer.

If you receive an offer from the company, you may have to respond in writing. If you accept the position, you may have certain conditions for that acceptance and they should be listed clearly in the letter. If you decide to reject the position, do it with the idea that you may want a position with that company at a later date. Your letter should be discrete about the reason for your rejection. You should respond to every communication you get from a company except for letters that say no position is open for someone with your qualifications at this time. These are basically form letters and do not require a response. Some sample letters follow.

Acceptance of Offer Letter

---

534 Highridge Ave.
Lake Forest, IL 43256
Jan 23, 1981

Ms. Patricia McCoy
Super Delux Tool Co.
444 Middle St.
Lake Forest, IL 43258

Dear Ms. McCoy:

    I am pleased to accept your offer of employment as Supervisor of the Data Entry Department at a salary of $23,500.

    I will give notice to my employer today and will report for work on February 9, 1981.

    I am looking forward to joining Super Delux.

                  Yours truly,

```
                                534 Highridge Ave.
                                Lake Forest, IL  43256
                                Jan 23, 1981

Mr. Hiram Walker
Acme Tool Co.
1456 Main St.
Lake Forest, IL  43256

Dear Mr. Walker:

    I have given careful consideration to your offer of a
position in the data processing department.  I have received
a number of other offers and have decided to accept one of
them.

    Thank you for the opportunity to learn about your
company.

                        Yours truly,
```

Rejection of Offer Letter

The appropriate form for a business letter, if you do not use a paper with a letter head, is shown here.

```
                                537 Maple Wood Drive
                                Fort Lauderdale, FL  33308
                                January 31, 1981

Mr. Paul Perfect
Director of Personnel
Prentice-Hall, Inc.
Englewood Cliffs, N.J.  07632

Dear Sir:
```

If you use paper with a letterhead, the appropriate form is:

```
                    LETTERHEAD COMPANY NAME
                    LETTERHEAD ADDRESS


                                        January 31, 1981

    Mr. Paul Perfect
    Director of Personnel
    Prentice-Hall, Inc.
    Englewood Cliffs, N.J.  07632

    Dear Sir:
```

The length of the résumé is dictated by its purpose and the amount of information you have to present. Although there is no single résumé format, specific areas should be covered. These include biographical information, education, professional goals, experience, military service, public offices held, publications, awards, etc. The arrangement of this information on the page or pages should be clear and easily referenced. There is no absolute format for this, but some suggested forms of résumés are presented in this chapter.

You may, in fact, need more than one form for your résumé. A very brief résumé is useful as an introduction or as an attachment to a presentation piece or portfolio. When I am submitting a proposal for a free-lance writing assignment to an editor who does not already know me, I generally attach a copy of what I call my Very Brief Résumé. It is not designed as a position-seeking piece.

VERY BRIEF RÉSUMÉ (no more than one page)

Biographical Information——Include name, address, home telephone number, and business telephone number.

Education——List colleges attended, year graduated, and degree(s) received. List advanced study, even if it did not lead to a degree, if it is relevant to the purpose of the résumé. Indicate school, year attended and the area studied. You may, for example, call it, "Additional course work in the field of...."

```
                    ANNA MAE WALSH BURKE
                    42 Bahama Lane
                    Pompano, Florida  33328
                    Work Telephone:  (305) 583-9872
                    Home Telephone:  (305) 491-2983
```

EDUCATION   Fordham University
                        Ph.D Degree - 1965 - Physics
                        M.S. Degree - 1962 - Physics
                  Manhattanville College
                        B.A. Degree - 1960 - Physics

EXPERIENCE
1979 --
Present Position

President, A & R Burke Corp., Fort Lauderdale, Florida Specialize in development of learning materials, assessment centers, assessment material, and computer learning systems software.

1974 to
Present

Director, Center for Science and Engineering, Nova University, Fort Lauderdale, Florida. Responsible for programs in Electrical Engineering, Computer Science, and Science and Mathematics.

1974 to 1981

Held a number of administrative positions at Nova University.

1963 to 1974

Held academic positions in universities and staff scientist positions in industry.

PUBLICATIONS
Books

The Plain Brown Wrapper Book of Microcomputers (to be published in 1981); Microcomputers for Writers (to be published in 1981); Microcomputers in the Classroom (with Robert Burke), Hayden Books (to be published in 1981); Computers Can Be Kidstuff, Hayden Books (1981); What Do You Want to Be Now That You're All Grown Up?, Prentice-Hall (1981); Are You Ready?: A Survival Manual for Women Returning to School, Prentice-Hall (1980); ten additional manuals and/or children's books.

```
PUBLICATIONS
(Continued)

Articles              Published forty technical articles
                      between 1964 and 1980; published in
                      national magazine New Woman in February
                      1981 issue.

BIOGRAPHICAL          Who's Who in America
LISTINGS              Who's Who in American Women
                      Who's Who in the South and Southeast
                      Dictionary of International Biography
                      American Catholic Who's Who
                      Men & Women of Distinction (International)
                      1980 Woman of the Year:  Broward County,
                         Florida (Education)
```

Very Brief Résumé

Goals——Goals should probably not be listed on this résumé. It is more of an introductory piece than a job-seeking instrument.

Experience——List your current position, if it is a fairly good one. Summarize your other positions and cover the years in large blocks, *e.g.:* 1970-1979—various administrative positions. If you are not working, and have not worked for a while, lump together the types of things you have done into a list or paragraph with a broad range of dates.

Military Service——Include military service only if it is pertinent or outstanding.

Public Service or Public Office——Include elected or appointed positions only if pertinent to purpose of the résumé or very beneficial to your reputation.

Publications and Presentations——Include recent publications (2 previous years) and summarize previous publications and presentations, e.g. fourteen professional papers published 1960-1980.

Awards——Include only if outstanding and pertinent to the purpose of the résumé.

THE SHORT RÉSUMÉ

The Very Brief Résumé is a promotional piece, but with the short résumé (no more than two pages!) you are trying to obtain a new position. Certain items above will be included or expanded.

Biographical Data——This section will remain as described for the Very Brief Résumé with the addition of marital information and number of children.

Education——This section will contain the information described in the Very Brief Résumé and some additional material. You should list professional study or special classes if relevant to the purpose of the résumé (such as art classes if you seek a job in art, study for special licenses, etc). Do not list your high school education unless you do not have any college, professional, or vocational study.

Goals——Because you are using this résumé to find a new position, you should include your job goals here. Do not limit them to a very specific position with one firm by name. Give a broader range of positions as your goal. Many individuals do not include any long-term goals, but there is some controversy about that. The person reviewing the résumé may think you will remain in the position for only a brief period if your goal is to move on to a more advanced position. An employer may not hire you because of this, but on the other hand, this may be just the reason you are hired. An employer may want someone with the initiative and skills which are needed for an advanced position. You will have to make this decision. It might depend on how important the long-range goal is to you.

Experience——This section will have to be expanded. You should list your current and previous positions with dates, company names and addresses, and a summary paragraph of your duties in these positions. If you do not have an extensive work background or if it is not relevant to the position you are seeking, you may need to add some "unpaid" work which may be relevant. If you have an extensive work history, present only the last ten years or four positions on this short résumé. Indicate other experiences in block form, *e.g.* 1955-1970 various positions in the retail industry. You will have to include volunteer or unpaid positions to expand this section in the direction of

```
CHARLES HARRIS
543 Maple Street
Miami, Florida  33290
Home Telephone:  (305) 987-6543
Married, three children

OBJECTIVE       A position of responsibility in a
                corporate training department that will
                allow me to train adults using
                techniques I have learned in education.

EDUCATION       Nova University
                  M.S. Degree - 1981 - Human Resource
                  Management
                Florida Atlantic University
                  B.S. Degree - 1972 - Education

EXPERIENCE
1975 to 1981    Dade County School System
                  Middle school science teacher in three
                  Date county middle schools.  Developed
                  self-instructional material for
                  students, a remedial mathematics
                  program for eighth grade students, and
                  a science club program in two schools.

MILITARY        United States Army
                  Infantry Officer in Viet Nam; Tactical
                  Training Officer, Fort Belvoir,
                  Virginia; highest rank held:  First
                  Lieutenant.
```

Short Résumé

your new career. You may have to focus on certain aspects of jobs you have held to give evidence of work in the new field. Do whatever you can to add relevant experience in this area.

Military Service——You may wish to include this section if it is not already included, or you may expand it.

Public Office——Include it if it is not included already.

Publications and Presentations——Expand your list to include more than just your last year's work. Do not hesitate to include reports which were circulated inside your company if you can prove that you did the work.

Awards——This may be expanded if the awards are important or if you have space enough to remain within the two page limit.

EXPANDED RÉSUMÉ

Biographical Data——You may add information about hobbies, interests, travel, languages spoken, etc. This will give the reviewer a more complete picture of you.

Goals——A more lengthy discussion may be included on this résumé.

Experience——You may include all the positions you have held and expand the listing of volunteer positions, especially if they are related to your new career goals.

Awards——You may find this is the best form on which to include your awards, rather than on the shorter résumé.

Two notes for all the résumés:

If you don't want your current employer to know you are seeking a new position, you should indicate this on your résumé and be discrete about receiving calls at your office. You may not want to type your letter on your company letterhead, although this does provide evidence of your present position.

Don't include the names of references on your résumé. You may indicate that references are available upon request. *Please* get permission from the individuals before you use their names, make certain they really know you, understand the type of position you are seeking, and be certain they will tell you what they will say. I have checked on people's references at times and discovered that the person can give only a bad reference or doesn't even remember the applicant.

The résumé is often the first and sometimes the only way you are represented to a prospective employer. Be certain that it represents you correctly. If you are moving into a completely new career area, add to your past work experience some examples of things you have done that will support the new career area. Draw on your educational background to reinforce this as well.

13

Selling yourself
—the interview

For some reason, I still remember the way I dressed for my first job interview (which, I might add, did lead to my first job). I wore a navy blue shirtwaist dress with a white collar, medium heels, nylon stockings, and carried white gloves. I had all the confidence which my seventeen years and the fact that I was going to college in the fall could give me. No matter how good or bad, the job, it was only temporary. I filled out an application, talked first to someone in the personnel department and then to the woman for whom I would work, and was hired.

The white gloves will give you a clue as to how long ago that job interview took place. The simplicity of the process I went through is almost as out of fashion as the white gloves. Of course, I was applying for only a low-paying job,—it probably was at the minimum wage. Obtaining a position at the professional level today often has all the simplicity of a NASA space launch compared to the process I went through on my first adventure in the world of work. Because obtaining a new position may involve several creative aspects, you may be more successful if you can get yourself "involved" rather than sitting back as if you consider yourself on trial. I realize that is much easier to write than to do.

Although interviewing can bring terror to the hearts of otherwise cool individuals, it is an important part of a career change. The fact that you have made it to the interview means that your résumé has survived some level of inspection. Now you will have to sell yourself to the interviewer. Interviewers understand your nervousness—they had to interview for their jobs also—but it is important to minimize it. This is especially true if the position you are seeking will be somewhat stressful.

In order to be successful at presenting yourself in a job-seeking session you have to realize the complexities of placement today for many professional level positions.

Hiring has become an extraordinarily complicated business phenomenon closely related to firing. Not only are there agencies specializing in placement, but some specialize in "outplacement" by helping individuals who have been terminated to face the future. I have done a great deal of hiring over the years and find that I am conscious more and more of the prospect of terminating someone, even during the initial interview. I find myself thinking what it would be like to terminate that person. It is almost like writing the divorce settlement as part of the marriage proposal process, but that also, apparently, is done today. There are so many federal regulations and lawsuits for one reason or another that the person doing the hiring has to take extraordinary measures to protect himself or herself in the hiring and firing processes. In most cases the interviewer, unless this is his or her profession, is not comfortable with the process of interviewing either. They are concerned that something will not be revealed in the interview that will ultimately result in a serious problem if the person is hired. The interview process, then, must produce a great deal more information than you might anticipate in order to ensure that sufficient data is available for the decision-making process. This leads to some very complex interview techniques, of which you must be aware if you are going to successfully compete in the career market.

In some cases, the hiring process has become extremely creative, as well as lengthy. One of my many hats is that of president of a corporation that develops assessment centers, among other things.

An assessment center is not a place, but a happening. It can happen with several hundred people or with a small number of interviewees for similar positions. It can happen in a few hours, it may take two or more consecutive days to be completed, or the sessions may be separated by various time periods.

The assessment center may include some kind of written testing on the part of the interviewee. If you go through one which has been developed by "The A. & R. Burke Corporation" it will contain several sessions in which you must perform some kind of job simulation activity and several group interaction activities. Many assessment centers contain some psychological testing and intelligence testing as well as some stress role playing. The real key to success in an assessment center is "letting yourself go," participating fully in the exercises.

If we review for a moment the process of developing a set of assessment center activities for a particular professional position, you may better understand the rationale behind the hiring process for that position.

First of all, the person or team who is doing the hiring generally is not certain of what they are doing. Certain questions are always present for them. "Am I selecting the right person?", "Does this person have some flaw I have overlooked?", "Is there some characteristic central to the position that I have overlooked?" If you understand where the interviewer is coming from, you will have a more successful interview.

When we are developing a "custom-tailored" assessment center, certain parameters must be established at the beginning, and this process often reveals some hidden agendas on the part of the individual(s) who will select the successful candidate. The characteristics required for the position must be determined by the group which is doing the hiring and these characteristics will often have little to do with the advertised requirements for the position. There will be certain minimum elements of education and experience which will be advertised or posted in a job bulletin. Those who are selecting the individual are interested in that person's ability to perform on the job, to be simultaneously a leader of others and a follower for them, if they are to be the supervisor. There will be individuals in the department with whom this person will have to interact and these will have "known" characteristics with which the person must interface. The person doing the hiring is interested in knowing the work habits of the interviewees. Are they able to learn new tasks quickly? Are they dependable? Are they imaginative? Different characteristics are important in different positions. Although many make this mistake, executives should not surround themselves with individuals who all have the same characteristics. Every company needs a successful mix of professionals. These characteristics are what must be revealed during the interview, or more rigorous assessment center, as well as the basic job knowledge.

Let us think your way through some basic elements of an interview. Although I did write that you should not act as though you think you are on trial, you are indeed being judged on the basis of the interview. You are being judged on the basis of your appearance and your behavior, on the basis of what you say and do, on your attitudes and expressions and on the basis of what you don't say or don't do. There is no right or wrong answer for which you can prepare before the interview in many instances. The person who hires you is the one who determines which answers are right or wrong with regard to a question. Think about it a moment, suppose you are able to fool the interviewer and tell him what you think he or she wants to hear. Suppose you present a self that is very different from what you are really like. Suppose you conceal a very different personality from the person who is hiring you. Are you going to want to perform in the new position in the resulting false manner that your superior is going to expect of you? Be careful not to fool yourself in this process. There are times, however, when you will find it necessary to present something in a manner that compensates for some unreasonable or predjudicial position on the part of the person conducting the interview.

Although there are no "right answers" you can learn ahead of time there are certain guidelines we can develop together that will be useful when preparing for an interview.

One very important aspect is knowledge of the company. You may not be able to find out a great deal about the position which is open but you will certainly be able to get information from books in the reference section of your library or from the personnel office of the company itself. Is it a large company, is it self-owned or part of a conglomerate? Does it have offices in other parts of the country? Is it related to other companies? How many employees does it have? How many years has the company been in business? What is the financial status of the company? Has it just had a reorganization or a merger?

These elements may be important in your final decision as to whether or not you will take the job, but they will also give you a knowledge base from which to work in your interview. Learn these things before you even apply to the company.

Suppose you are called for an interview. Your education and experience have probably already been identified in the résumé. If you are seeking a career position, these characteristics will already have been reviewed in a screening process. This process may have been separated from the interview by only a short period of time or by several weeks, but this differentiation in time will generally exist.

Let us assume there will be one or more interviews which you will have to successfully complete for a certain position, but that there is not a formal assessment center. There are many components for which you will have to be prepared.

You must agree with yourself—you are trying to get a position, not make a social statement. This may seem to be a ridiculous statement, but many people lose touch with their purpose in the process of establishing something else, such as an excuse for not getting the position, or to satisfy an unconscious fear that they will get the job but not be able to perform. A man who will not get a haircut or wear a tie, a woman who wears tight pants or a plunging neckline to an interview for a business position is not thinking about winning that position. They are trying to make a social statement, and perhaps are subconsciously setting up a defense for rejection by not playing by the rules.

Your appearance is very important and must be correlated to the position you are seeking. This may or may not change according to the area of the country in which the position is located. People from outside of the state are often not aware of the fact that most professional people in Florida dress in the same manner as people in New York except for the absence of wool in the fabric. They seem to believe that cruise wear is the order of the day here in business offices, but this is not true. Study not only what is being worn in the general industry to which you are applying for a position, but in that particular company.

Some colleges and companies are very "tweedy," while others are characterized by business suits. I do not use the term "suit" with only respect to men. The acceptance of the skirted suit, the ensemble or the jacketed dress as a uniform for the professional woman, has been very rapid. A tailored dress may also be worn, especially in warmer weather, but everywhere I go I see suits.

The first impression you make on the interviewer is with your appearance. Although the specific items of clothing will obviously be different, some of the standards will be the same for both men and women. Unless the position has a special characteristic that must be taken into account—such as the lead singer in a rock band—you should dress fairly conservatively in quiet, well-fitting clothing. A suit, skirted for women, is always a good choice. If the weather is warm, women may wear tailored dresses, but men should still wear suits. I do realize that there is a movement away from the suit as a newly-found uniform for women but it is still a good choice for a job interview. Although a sports jacket might be acceptable in some situations, matching pants and jacket will be generally more effective. Colors should also be conservative unless you have some very good reason for choosing something else. Attractive applicants are selected more often than those who are unattractive.

Please note that I did not say *beautiful*.... Not everyone can be beautiful, and standards for beauty are different. Most people can be *attractive*, however. Such things as good haircuts and attractive, business-like hairdos, well-fitting, appropriate, well-coordinated clothing in fairly neutral colors and well-kept shoes add to that attractive image. A woman's make-up will be determined partly by what she generally wears. It should not look as though she were going out for the evening after the interview, but I have never subscribed to the theory that a woman in business should wear no make-up. I have always believed that make-up should be attractive but not obvious. As mentioned in the previous section on appearance, things like dandruff on the shoulder or broken, dirty fingernails loom large in an interview, although, they are totally unimportant in most work situations. You create an image in an interview. Be certain that your appearance adds to that image.

There may be one or more interviewers. In the latter case, the interview will be more complex, but the things you must remember will be the same. When considering an interview, I cannot help but remember some of the techniques the police are said to use when questioning suspects. The typical TV scene will be a poorly-lit room in the station house with a naked bulb hanging from the ceiling. One detective will be nasty, relentlessly questioning the suspect; the other will be the good guy who will interfere and play the role of friend to the criminal. The criminal responds to the kindness by telling the nice officer where he hid the body or the jewels, etc.

Interviewers don't play quite the same games, but they are dedicated to getting you to reveal things about yourself that you don't want to reveal. You may believe that you will not reveal these things, but the skilled interviewers can get you to do it. Remember, you won't give a good interview if you do not interact to some degree. You cannot just answer with a monosyllabic "yes" or "no" or "I don't know." You should be aware of this if there is a particular skeleton you want to keep in your closet. In a recent assessent center we were planning, one of the people from the company told us that he was going to use a psychological evaluation in addition to the material we had developed. This apparently was designed to reveal all sorts of things, such as whether or not the person being considered was an alcoholic. It seemed a little extreme to all of us, but this was what the psychologist had told the company he could obtain through his evaluations. I include this only to give you a sense of the kind of things companies are worried about.

Many locations can be used for interviewing, depending on the level of the position, but some, if not all of the interview will be in an office. If the person who is doing the interview does not come out of the office or at least to the door of the office to greet you, take it as a general indicator that the position is not a very high one, regardless of the title. There are three general seating patterns in most offices, and the choice is up to the interviewer. Do not assume a seat until you see where the interviewer will sit. The three patterns are:

1. The interviewer sits at his or her desk. You sit in a chair in front or at the side of the desk. If the interviewer assumes a seat at the desk and there is no chair near the desk, ask if you can move one to a convenient position. If there is blinding sunlight in your eyes, move your chair slightly. The situation may be staged to see if you have initiative—have some, but don't have so much that you take the boss's chair.

2. You both sit at a table. This format will be more relaxing than having the interviewer at the desk, because you will be in a peer simulation role here. In the previous example, the desk established the pecking order immediately. You could not doubt for a minute who was "boss," who was in charge. At the position at the table, the seating pattern does not establish who is in charge unless there is a very definite "head of the table" position. Many people have round tables in their offices so that role definition will not be predetermined by the seating. Again, see where the interviewer sits and select a seat from which you can talk clearly without having to sit at an awkward angle.

3. The third position is one in which you have comfortable chairs and/or a comfortable sofa. Again your position is dictated by the

position which the interviewer takes. If he/she chooses the chair, sit on the end of the sofa which is nearest the chair. If he/she choses the sofa, don't sit next to him/her. Sit on the other piece of furniture. This arrangement is intended to make you feel very relaxed.

After you have chosen your position, think about the way you are sitting. Body language is extremely important. Your body language may be signalling things you wouldn't dream of saying. What you do with your hands and feet is probably the most important thing. Figitting, moving excessivly, or tapping your hands or feet may indicate that you are terribly nervous. Never play with your face, your nose, your ears, your hair, etc. Try not to touch them at all. Don't play with jewelry or watches either, and for heaven's sake, don't look at your watch. Time should not be important to you in the middle of an interview. You may be signalling that the interview is a waste of time to you or that you have something better to do, like another interview, and are running late.

There are generally four stages to an interview. The warm-up time during which you and the interviewer become comfortable with each other is first. Although this is important, don't get so carried away with friendliness that you forget you are there to obtain a position to begin your new career.

During the second stage, you and the interviewer will exchange information. The way you phrase the information you give the interviewer will be part of your selling job. You can reveal some of your knowledge about the company during this process. Choose your words to maximize the things you tell about yourself. Don't talk too much, but don't resort to monosylables either.

The third stage usually focuses on a specific position or on a general area of positions. Don't hesitate to appear interested if you are. Remaining reserved at this point may give the interviewer the idea that you are not interested in the position. Don't be afraid to inquire about such details as salary at this point. People sometimes are reluctant to discuss money, but this is an important part of any position. Certain things should be left until a specific offer is made. You don't need to discuss the retirement package when you are in the middle of a first interview. You should, however, discuss it before you finally take the position along, with the question of raises and promotion policy, medical benefits, educational benefits and other things which will concern you if you take the posiiton. Terminating the interview can be a somewhat difficult process. Try to be confident. Ask any questions which you may still have and watch for the cues that the interviewer considers the interview to be over. You now know more about each other than when you began the interview, and the leave-taking may be friendlier than the beginning. Of course, if the interview didn't go well it may be even more strained. It is sometimes difficult to know that you are the cause of any tenseness on the part of the interviewer. It may be the garlic he had for lunch or the meeting he is on his way to with his boss which causes him to have a sour look. Don't forget to send the thank-you letter.

While the four stages seem simple enough, there are a number of do's and don't's to be remembered.

Don't get caught up in telling stories or anecdotes. You should talk of course and do more than just give monosylabic answers to the questions which you are asked, but don't get carried away in little stories. This is especially symptomatic of women returning to work after a long absence. It is perhaps more accepted with men who traditionally tell old war stories. To some degree you have to follow the lead of the interviewer.

If you have a friend who will role play with you, use him or her to check you out for your body language and habits. Arrange set-ups for an interview using the three seating patterns described above. Have the person ask you all sorts of questions and note your responses. While your friend may not be able to judge the effectiveness of your responses, he or she will be able to take note of all the things you do that may add or subtract from the interview.

Don't have garlic or onions for lunch. Don't have a beer or a drink, either. Don't wear strong perfume and don't smoke unless the interviewer invites you to.

While I do of course encourage honesty, there is a limit to what the interviewer is entitled to know. Certain questions may be discriminatory, which is a violation of the law. You do not have to answer these types of questions and can say as much in the nicest of terms.

In spite of the illegality of it, some interviewers do not hesitate to ask questions about your age or, in the case of women, if you are expecting a baby. You do not have to answer these questions, but it is not necessarily advisable to bang the interviewer over the head with the illegality of the questions. Discrimination is a reality in spite of the laws. You must fight it, but the interview room is not always the place. Answer no question you do not want to answer or to which the interviewer is not entitled to an answer. Just don't get rowdy about it.

Because you will be either changing careers or returning to work after a number of years' absence, you will undoubtedly be asked why you are looking for the job for which you are being interviewed. There may be questions about gaps in your employment record or about your selection of the new field. While the interviewer may indeed be looking for answers to which he or she is not legally entitled, the questions are natural. You never know, the questioner may be looking for a new career himself. Do not be overly sensitive about such questions, and prepare in advance a response that satisfies you.

Sometimes the interviewer may ask questions that seem to come out of our old friend, the *Dictionary of Occupational Titles*... Are you interested in people, places or things? Will you be able to travel? Do you like to travel?

Other questions seem to have been gleaned up from a final exam. What kind of a boss do you like to work for, or alternately, what style of leadership do you like to assume? What are your strengths, what are your weaknesses? Do you like "detail work?" If you could have any job in the company, what would you choose? Why? What are your career goals? What plans have you for the next five years? Ten years? If you could change anything in the company what would it be?

Sometimes the interviewer will ask you about something on your application which is of interest to him personally. It may be a hobby you have, or a trip you have taken, or the place where you were born or went to school. In South Florida, for example, we always ask people where they are from when we meet them. In New York we generally talked about the transportation you take to work and the hardship you experience (subway breakdowns, LIRR strikes etc.). In Boston, although my contacts may have been too narrow, the conversation seemed to run to skiing, sailing, being stuck on the bridge to Cape Cod and remodeling old houses. I am certain that other areas have their favorite questions. Remember that in the case of the interviewer who will be your boss rather than a professional interviewer, the interviewer may also be a little nervous and may be trying to make some small talk to relax both of you.

You have to remember that not all interviewers are nice. The person doing the interview may have many discriminatory attitudes. He or she may want a person who is clearly identified as being the traditional "type" for the position and reject applicants who do not fit a pre-set idea.

The person who is changing careers, especially at midlife, or is coming back into a profession after a lengthy absence generally does not fit a pre-set model. There may be many rather pointed questions directed toward them. Some of these questions may be very insulting, such as:

1. What happened, didn't you do well in your other field?
2. Do you think you will be able to get back in the swing after your long vacation? (Raising four children is some vacation.)
3. What makes you think you can do this job? (A degree in the field and work experience in other areas.)
4. Aren't you a little old to be trying something new?
5. This isn't a retirement position, you know.
6. I suppose you are going to have to take a lot of time off to take care of your children?
7. What do you think about women's lib?
8. Did your wife talk you into getting a new job...?

You may find yourself in the position of having to find a response to questions which are just as improper and just as rudely asked as the previous samples. Although you may be quite angry about the whole situation, you will also have to be ready to respond. One technique is to take your résumé and your life situation (man or woman, in a new career or returning to work, etc.) and make a list of all the nasty questions that could be asked. Sort these into categories such as age, gaps in your résumé, the fact that you are changing careers, your choice of the new career, selection of the particular position, health, family responsibilities etc. You should prepare general categories of reponses to these questions. Refusal to answer, of course, may be one of your choices. Remember, no matter how angry discrimination may make you, you are trying to get a position, not win a battle. You do that after you get the position.

While the interview is generally considered to be a period in which questions are asked of you, you can use it to find out some things about the position for which you are applying. Many interviewers will not necessarily know all the details concerning the health and retirement plans which will apply to you, or the policy on vacations or personal days for people in your category. They may not even know the exact salary scheduled for the position, but it does no harm to ask. If the interviewer will be your supervisor, you may ask questions about the work, possibly using the job description as well as questions about the way in which you will function in the office, and about your relationship to the people with whom you will be working. This is information you will need before you can make a decision to accept the position if it is offered. You should not seem overly concerned about a particular aspect of the position that you do not care for, or the interviewer may become negative toward you. Wait until you are offered the position and then negotiate the aspects of the position that displease you. You will be in a better position to do so at that time.

Now I am going to tell you to do the impossible, *relax*.... Everybody is nervous in an interview to some degree, but the higher the level of the position, the more relaxed and in control you must seem. Although you must be relaxed, you must simultaneously try to be aware of the impact every move you make and every word you say will have on the interviewer. This is certainly an impossible undertaking, but it is the task that has been set for you.

It is often said that you get a job offer (and the same goes for a new position) when you are not looking for it and this is indeed often true. The point is that you are relaxed when you are not looking for a new position, while this is certainly not the case if you care very much whether you get it. This caring may make you so nervous that you eliminate yourself from the competition.

Stress is a fact of the modern world and the person who is going to survive will have to be able to handle it well. If you cannot function in the interview, the interviewer may well be justified in assuming that you will not be able to survive in the new job. Minimize your stress by mentally acting out many of the steps you will go through ahead of time.

14

What if they make an offer?

Ironically, the next to the worst thing to *not* getting an offer is getting one and having to make a decision. Selecting that first position when you are attempting to make a career change is a difficult decision. You have decided to make the change and have gone out and sought a new position. You are probably still asking yourself the question "Am I doing the right thing?" Now you have to ask not only this, but also, "Is this the right job?" If only we were blessed with the ability to see the future once in a while, such questions might be simplified. They might also be complicated by our seeing things which depress us.

Selecting a new job is a little bit like selecting a marriage partner. Is this the right person? If you wait will a better choice come along? Just as many people are left waiting for the right knight or princess to come riding along, applicants frequently are left waiting for the right position to open up. On the other hand, many decide too quickly, and take a position just because it was available. I always wonder about a certain position I once accepted when another seemed impossible to get. I had signed a contract for the first position, and the one I preferred was offered to me a few weeks later. I did not want to break a contract, but I have always wondered what would have happened in my life if I had taken the second position. Perhaps it would have been better, perhaps it would not. But I will never know. Life is full of "what ifs." The important thing is to make the best possible decision using all the information at your disposal. Don't let inertia set in. Don't let fear stop you and don't spend your days saying "If only. . . ."

There really is no way to be certain whether you should take a particular position or not. The answer will be different in each person's case. There are, however, a number of questions you can ask yourself. You will have to base your final judgment on the answers to these and any other questions you can think of. In the end, you will have to make the final decision on the basis of your intuition . . . your feelings. There is an element of luck in every choice and in every decision you make. The key question seems to be concerned not only with the "present" of the job but also with its "future."

Travelers Insurance Company has an ad describing a gentleman who turned down a position with the newly founded insurance company in 1864. Looking back, the ad claims, the gentleman appears to have been shortsighted. Worried about the economy, he kept his job selling blacksmith supplies. I'm not so certain that he was shortsighted. Not everyone is emotionally prepared to take risks. Perhaps selling blacksmith supplies was the best position for him at that time.

Selecting the new position can only be made after a great deal of soul searching. Ask yourself some of the following questions:

1. Does the position seem to have a future?
2. Will it lead me to the next step on my projected career ladder?
3. Will the position give me good experience?
4. Does the company have a good reputation?
5. Does the salary seem fair for the position considering my experience and education?
6. Do I like the environment in which I will be working?
7. Do I think I can do the work?
8. Will I "feel good" about doing the work or having that title or position?
9. What is the reaction of my family to the job offer?
10. Will I have to travel, work overtime or unusual hours?
11. Is the position the kind of work I have been seeking?
12. Will it give me an opportunity to "get in" to a company which could provide me with the kind of position I really seek?

13. Will I have to move?
14. Will I be able to continue my educational program?
15. Do I have any prospects with other companies which might fit better with my goals?
16. Have I been out of work and therefore need the job?
17. Will the specific tasks which I will have to do for the position interest me? Will I be quickly bored?
18. How will I get to the new job? Is the commute impossible?
19. What will I do if I don't take the position?
20. If I turn down this position do I think the company will make me an offer for the job I want at a later date?
21. What other job in that company would I prefer?
22. What other job in that company am I qualified for?
23. Are there any other immediate prospects?
24. Will working in this position for a while enable me to get the job I want with another company?

You may want to review some of the problems you have had with jobs in the past. How can you avoid having them repeated in the new position? Are they likely to reappear if you take this position?

What do your family and friends think about the offer? Discuss it with those individuals whom you know are not jealous of you or opposed to your change of careers. Do they understand you pretty well? Are they sympathetic to your goals?

Suppose you have had two interviews with companies. Both seem promising. For some reason you would prefer the position at Company A, but the offer comes first from Company B. There is no way that you can put off giving Company B an immediate answer. What do you do besides chewing your nails, that is?

There are several schools of thought on this question.

1. You can accept the offer from company B. An offer in the hand is worth two in the bush. Sometimes this is true. The second offer may never come.
2. You can turn down the offer from Company B and wait for the offer from Company A. It may not come but, again, it may come.
3. You can try to get a little time from Company B in order to give them an answer. Remember that they won't like thinking they were your second choice and you may be jeoparizing your future at company B.
4. You can talk to the person from Company A and indicate that you have a viable offer from another company, that you would be

interested in considering an offer from them and that you wonder if they are going to make such an offer to you soon.

This may blow all of your chances with company A but if you were going to take company B's offer anyway, that won't matter. It may push Company A into making an offer to you or they may decide they don't want to compete. They may have decided not to make you an offer anyway. This would be suicidal to try if you didn't have a genuine offer of a position you wanted from Company B.

After you have made the decision to take the new position you will have to give notice to your current company. Although you may be relieved to be leaving your present position, you cannot make that apparent. You will need references from that position for many years. Be sure to leave them with adequate notice and on good terms. Don't tell your boss off, for example. Get a letter of recommendation before you leave. It may be useful later.

Mentally prepare yourself for the new position. Have problems arisen in other positions you have held over the years? Have you had problems with co-workers, bosses, punctuality or other things? Think about these things honestly and try to avoid the same problems in your new position. Beginning a new career won't solve your problems if you fall back into patterns that have caused problems for you before.

It will be important for you to fit into the new position while being identified for your abilities. This means fitting in with the people with whom you will be working. It means looking as though you belong in the company. You may need some new items in your wardrobe to look the part you must play in the new position. It means learning your new job quickly and acting with confidence. A willingness to learn is an important asset to bring to your new position.

You should bring to your first position in your new career a fresh outlook and enthusiasm. Act with the confidence that comes with years of experience, even though it may have been in a different position. You should be excited. It is a fresh future for you and for your family.

15

Becoming your own boss

For many, the selection of a new career is linked to the desire to become their own boss.

Those who become writers or enter into one of the arts or crafts experience this to some degree. Their experience as bosses, however, is simplified by the fact that they are generally their only employee.

The relationship is more directly experienced by those who decide to open their own businesses. This subject is extremely complex and will only be discussed briefly in this chapter. If you are considering opening a business as your new career, I recommend that you read some of the books that have been published on the matter. The government has several booklets on small businesses and offers workshops in many areas on concerns like keeping tax records. If you are considering starting your own business or buying someone else's, you might be interested in going to some of these workshops in advance to understand just what you are getting into.

Each year thousands of businesses open, and each year thousands close. They are not necessarily the same businesses, of course. In today's economy it is very difficult to successfully start a business. If this is your choice for a second career, go cautiously and be aware of all the demands it will make on you.

Time—that monster that controls our lives—will be of particular importance when you start a new business. Suddenly you will not only be the boss, but you may be all or most of all of the employees.

You may find yourself doing many tasks, and some of them may be ones you sought to escape. The boss in a new company rarely works decent hours. Being a boss is not a nine to five job. If you don't do the task yourself, you will have to pay someone to do it, and that brings us to the second point for discussion.

Money is a serious topic today. The cost of borrowing money has caused changes in the way many companies, even large corporations, do business. Some very large concerns, for example, no longer accept credit cards. If you are going to start a business you will need to have sufficient capital available, in spite of the high cost of borrowing. Insufficient capital or an inability to maintain inventory has caused businesses to fold—businesses that would have been successful if they could have weathered various crises.

If you are going to open a store that will either be based on your own talents and products or those of others, you will have to pay close attention to location. People are conscious of both safety and travel time these days, and no one will beat a path to anybody's door any more no matter how good the mousetrap. A good location will undoubtedly be expensive, but may be a necessity for success.

Federal and state tax laws will demand a great deal of attention on your part. There are requirements for workman's compensation and health insurance policies, and other benefits which you will have to follow. You will either have to keep your own books and tax records or hire an accountant to do it. The number of forms you have to submit seems to increase yearly. Not filing the correct form at the right time can bring about penalties.

If you are going to work in a business with other members of your family, be certain that you can work together on this basis. Such endeavors have brought trouble to formerly peaceful families. Family businesses have been the backbone of this country, but you should be aware of anticipated difficulties and try to solve problems before they start. Being the boss may result in family strife.

Although I may sound negative, I don't mean to be. I have seen a number of people try to start businesses without sufficient capital and without realizing how much time it would take from their lives. I wish to caution you to watch for the pitfalls. Having your own business can be the most satisfying experience, and it can also bring you great fortune that cannot be matched by salary. It can bring you considerable pride and satisfaction and it may be work that you like. You can always make yourself president. It can be a great experience, but it also can be a disaster.

If you are seriously considering starting your own business, plan those aspects we have discussed—the time, the money, the location, the regulations, and the opportunities. Can you do it all? It may be years before your business shows a profit. That is not a mark of failure, but is common for new businesses. Can you exist without any real income for a year or two while you are simultaneously putting money into the company? These are important questions, ones which you must answer before you take the final steps and establish yourself as *boss*.

Remember that the man or woman who works for him/herself has a difficult boss.

16

Don't Stop Now

You have taken the first step. You have begun to think about a new career. It is possible for you, it is possible for everyone. We only live once and it is important to get some satisfaction from daily experiences. It is important to have pride in yourself and what you do for a living.

You may be forced to find a new position because your present work area is being phased out by technology. You may have identified a new career area that did not exist in earlier years. You may be thinking about pursuing a dream you have had since childhood. Study the career area carefully. Find a position in that area for which you can prepare yourself.

You may have identified certain training you will need in order to obtain the position you want within the new career area. You may have to make adjustments in your family life for a period of time. You may have to take a temporary cut in income or you may have to increase your workload. You may have to ask others for help. You may have to borrow money. You may have to go back to school. You may have to do many things that will be hard for you, but the final goal will be worth it.

You took the first step when you picked up this book. *Don't stop now.*

Appendix

EXPLANATION OF DATA, PEOPLE, AND THINGS

Much of the information in this publication is based on the premise that every job requires a worker to function in some degree to *data, people,* and *things.*[1] These relationships are identified and explained below. They appear in the form of three listings arranged in each instance from the relatively simple to the complex in such a manner that each successive relationship includes those that are simpler and excludes the more complex.[2] The identifications attached to these relationships are referred to as *worker functions,* and provide standard terminology for use in summarizing exactly what a worker does on the job.

A job's relationship to *data, people,* and *things* can be expressed in terms of the lowest numbered function in each sequence. These functions taken

---

[1]This section has been taken from *The Dictionary of Occupational Titles,* 4th edition, printed 1977 by the U.S. Department of Labor, Division of Employment and Training.

[2]As each of the relationships to *people* represents a wide range of complexity, resulting in considerable overlap among occupations, their arrangement is somewhat arbitrary and can be considered a hierarchy only in the most general sense.

together indicate the total level of complexity at which the worker performs. The fourth, fifth and sixth digits of the occupational code numbers reflect relationships to *data, people,* and *things,* respectively.[3] These digits express a job's relationship to *data, people,* and *things* by identifying the highest appropriate function in each listing as reflected by the following table:

DATA (4th digit)	*PEOPLE (5th digit)*	*THINGS (6th digit)*
1 Synthesizing	0 Mentoring	0 Setting-Up
1 Coordinating	1 Negotiating	1 Precision Working
2 Analyzing	2 Instructing	2 Operating-Controlling
3 Compiling	3 Supervising	3 Driving-Operating
4 Computing	4 Diverting	4 Manipulating
5 Copying	5 Persuading	5 Tending
6 Comparing	6 Speaking-Signaling	6 Feeding-Offbearing
	7 Serving	7 Handling
	8 Taking Instructions-Helping	

DEFINITIONS OF WORKER FUNCTIONS

DATA: Information, knowledge, and conceptions related to data, people, or things, obtained by observation, investigation, interpretation, visualization, and mental creation. Data are intangible and include numbers, words, symbols, ideas, concepts, and oral verbalization.

0. Synthesizing: Integrating analyses of data to discover facts and/or develop knowledge concepts or interpretations.
1. Coordinating: Determining time, place, and sequence of operations or action to be taken on the basis of analysis of data; executing determination and/or reporting on events.
2. Analyzing: Examining and evaluating data. Presenting alternative actions in relation to the evaluation is frequently involved.

---

[3]Only those relationships which are occupationally significant in terms of the requirements of the job are reflected in the code numbers. The incidental relationships which every worker has to *data, people,* and *things,* but which do not seriously affect successful performance of the essential duties of the job, are not reflected.

3. Compiling: Gathering, collating, or classifying information about data, people, or things. Reporting and/or carrying out a prescribed action in relation to the information is frequently involved.

4. Computing: Performing arithmetic operations and reporting on and/or carrying out a prescribed action in relation to them. Does not include counting.

5. Copying: Transcribing, entering, or posting data.

6. Comparing: Judging the readily observable functional, structural, or compositional characteristics (whether similar to or divergent from obvious standards) of data, people, or things.

PEOPLE: Human beings; also animals dealt with on an individual basis as if they were human.

0. Mentoring: Dealing with individuals in terms of their total personality in order to advise, counsel, and/or guide them with regard to problems that may be resolved by legal, scientific, clinical, spiritual, and/or other professional principles.

1. Negotiating: Exchanging ideas, information, and opinions with others to formulate policies and programs and/or arrive jointly at decisions, conclusions, or solutions.

2. Instructing: Teaching subject matter to others, or training others (including animals) through explanation, demonstration, and supervised practice; or making recommendations on the basis of technical disciplines.

3. Supervising: Determining or interpreting work procedures for a group of workers, assigning specific duties to them, maintaining harmonious relations among them, and promoting efficiency. A variety of responsibilities is involved in this function.

4. Diverting: Amusing others. (Usually accomplished through the medium of stage, screen, television, or radio.)

5. Persuading: Influencing others in favor of a product, service, or point of view.

6. Speaking-Signaling: Talking with and/or signaling people to convey or exchange information. Includes giving assignments and/or directions to helpers or assistants.

7. Serving: Attending to the needs or requests of people or animals or the expressed or implicit wishes of people. Immediate response is involved.

8. Taking Instructions-Helping: Helping applies to "non-learning" helpers. No variety of responsibility is involved in this function.

THINGS: Inanimate objects as distinguished from human beings, substances or materials; machines, tools, equipment and products. A thing is tangible and has shape, form, and other physical characteristics.

0. Setting up: Adjusting machines or equipment by replacing or altering tools, jigs, fixtures, and attachments to prepare them to perform their functions, change their performance, or restore their proper functioning if they break down. Workers who set up one or a number of machines for other workers or who set up and personally operate a variety of machines are included here.

1. Precision Working: Using body members and/or tools or work aids to work, move, guide, or place objects or materials in situations where ultimate responsibility for the attainment of standards occurs and selection of appropriate tools, objects, or materials, and the adjustment of the tool to the task require exercise of considerable judgment.

2. Operating-Controlling: Starting, stopping, controlling, and adjusting the progress of machines or equipment. Operating machines involves setting up and adjusting the machine or material(s) as the work progresses. Controlling involves observing gages, dials, etc., and turning valves and other devices to regulate factors such as temperature, pressure, flow of liquids, speed of pumps, and reactions of materials.

3. Driving-Operating: Starting, stopping, and controlling the actions of machines or equipment for which a course must be steered, or which must be guided, in order to fabricate, process, and/or move things or people. Involves such activities as observing gages and dials; estimating distances and determining speed and direction of other objects; turning cranks and wheels; pushing or pulling gear lifts or levers. Includes such machines as cranes, conveyor systems, tractors, furnace charging machines, paving machines and hoisting machines. Excludes manually powered machines, such as handtrucks and dollies, and power assisted machines, such as electric wheelbarrows and handtrucks.

4. Manipulating: Using body members, tools, or special devices to work, move, guide, or place objects or materials. Involves some latitude for judgment with regard to precision attained and selecting appropriate tool, object, or material, although this is readily manifest.

5. Tending: Starting, stopping, and observing the functioning of machines and equipment. Involves adjusting materials or controls of the machine, such as changing guides, adjusting timers and temperature gages, turning valves to allow flow of materials, and flipping switches in response to lights. Little judgment is involved in making these adjustments.

6. Feeding-Offbearing: Inserting, throwing, dumping, or placing materials in or removing them from machines or equipment which are automatic or tended or operated by other workers.

7. Handling: Using body members, handtools, and/or special devices to work, move or carry objects or materials. Involves little or no latitude for judgment with regard to attainment of standards or in selecting appropriate tool, object, or material.

Index